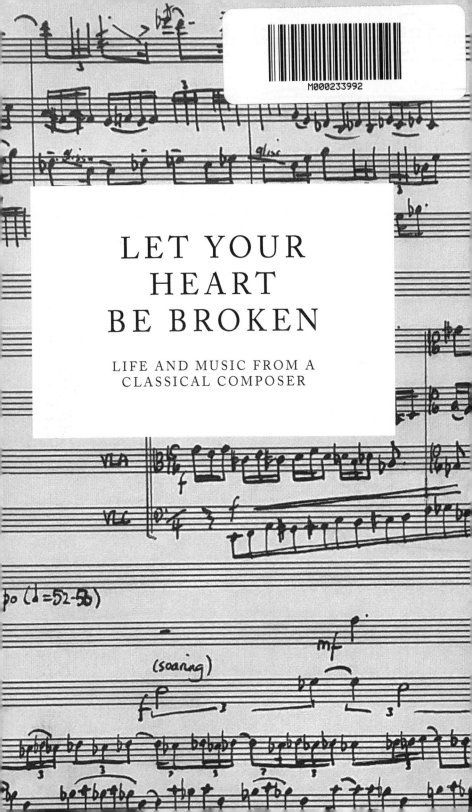

LET YOUR HEART BE BROKEN

LIFE AND MUSIC FROM A CLASSICAL COMPOSER

LET YOUR HEART BE BROKEN

LIFE AND MUSIC FROM A CLASSICAL COMPOSER

TINA DAVIDSON

Boyle
&
Dalton

Book Design & Production:
Boyle & Dalton
www.BoyleandDalton.com

Paperback ISBN: 978-1-63337-696-0
Hardback ISBN: 978-1-63337-697-7
E-book ISBN: 978-1-63337-698-4

Printed in the United States of America
1 3 5 7 9 10 8 6 4 2

For my daughter, Cassandra

CONTENTS

AUTHOR'S NOTE

I am a composer. I delight in the ebb and flow of energy, the gathering of melodies and rhythmic passages, and the shaping of them into a continuously moving sound. Often there is a slightly off-balance forward movement; the moment of arrival is a departure, with the final destination an arc swirling upward.

I have always kept both personal and music journals. The practice, starting in adolescence, became a daily routine in my composing life. My workday began with reading and then writing for an hour or more before turning to my compositions. At times I wrote casually; other times I wrote as if to save my life.

To create this memoir, I relied heavily on memory and family stories of my childhood, and I pulled from my journals (1986–1997), editing for clarity. These I piece together side by side like patchwork—my growing up next to my artistic process, my evolving understanding of my life and origins next to the music I create. Both are an act of placing and grounding. Writing, however, is more vulnerable, truer to life's storytelling. Composing is in a world of its own—both emotion and energy; I camouflage myself, wrap myself in a language that has no direct translation. Writing reveals me naked.

I have changed the names of some but not all the individuals in this book.

TINA DAVIDSON

An audience member stands. "What is the meaning of life?" he asks.

Stephen Levine, author, poet best known for his work on death and dying, sits on the large stage looking down at a hundred expectant faces. I am at the Open Center in New York City at a two-day seminar.

He relaxes back into his chair. "I am asked that all the time," he replies, his voice burnishing the microphone, "and I really don't know." He pauses, looking to the side. He turns back, smiling. "But I think the meaning of life is to let your heart be broken."

The heart, the round sphere of your being. Let your heart be broken. Allow, expect, look forward to. The life that you have so carefully protected and cared for. Broken, cracked, rent in two. Heartbreakingly, your heart breaks, and in the two halves, rocking on the table, is revealed rich earth. Moist, dark soil, ready for new life to begin.

Overture

MEMORY'S PASSAGE

The way back into memory is circuitous. The path crisscrosses, dead ends, starts up again, and changes directions. Darkness opens up to light, colors kaleidoscope, and shapes are broken into a thousand patterns.

The past presses on the present with staggering consistency. Nothing is separate or fresh, always an afterimage. The slow time-lapse photograph catches the multi-image movement of our lives. Danger lurks in every corner. To reconstruct will challenge perceptions of self, to restore will allow old pain to well up.

The price of forgotten memories, however, is more costly. My puppeteer of darkness is cruel. He perpetuates false beliefs and forces reenactments I cannot control.

The miracle is light. The miracle is that we rise again out of suffering. The miracle is the persistence of the soul to find itself, to look hard into the darkness, reach back, and grasp remnants of ourselves. The miracle is that we create ourselves anew.

5

As I look back at all of this now, my daughter was my great opportunity. Born on a cold Thanksgiving Wednesday in 1984, Cassie was a beautiful compact shape and came without complications. I spent the holiday in the Philadelphia hospital grateful and humble.

Wood and I were delighted new parents—earnest, starry-eyed, arrogant, and foolish. Together we measured every change, smiling indulgently at each other. I nursed with great abundance; Cassie preferred one side, and I grew happily unbalanced. I was writing music that felt rich and authentic, pleasing me for the first time that I could remember. A cello concerto for the Sage City Symphony was my first paid commission, and the melodies soared, the rhythms snapped. The garden was full of flowers, the sun was hot. In the early mornings, I lay in my airy bedroom filled with soft blue light, snuggled next to this little form, breath to breath.

In truth, my life was falling apart. My close friendships were angry and blistering. My relationship with my sister Eva, who, with her husband, had come down to live in the upstairs apartment, erupted. Amid the joy, my life was teetering, and I couldn't understand why. The structure I had built creaked and swayed. I woke at night in a rage and fought battles with phantoms. I obsessively sorted through arguments, wrote long letters, destroyed them, only to write them again.

The only quiet I had was when I nursed my daughter. Her plump hand reached up, stroked my neck, and twirled my hair. We were peacefully one.

I could descend into forgetfulness and depression as I had done so many times in the past, or I could put my hands and heart to work. Her small life hung in the balance.

I sat in the therapist's basement office. She tapped a pencil against her notebook, thinking. *This is ridiculous*, I told myself, promising to stop therapy at the end of the session. The afternoon was beginning to darken, and the rows of casement windows were full of shadows.

"Tell me that dream," she encouraged me again, "as if you were dreaming it now." With a sigh I allowed my eyes to close and relax. I had only twenty minutes left in the session. I could manage this last task.

My nights had always been haunted by dreams of damaged houses and silent, empty rooms, of basements moist with dark lagoons, of sleek black dogs tugging at my pant leg, and of dangerous men lurking in alleys. But the most vivid, persistent dream, one I'd had since I was three years old, was of an elevator. Once the doors closed, it tipped precariously to the side, stopping between floors, opening finally to a dark hallway. The silence was leaden. Closed apartment doors stretched off out of sight. I awoke gasping and sickened.

"Why don't you get off and walk down the hallway?" she suggested.

I step out tentatively. The hall curves. The carpet is old and scuffed, the walls are gray. I slide my hand on the cool plaster as I walk past closed door after closed door. Suddenly a door is open; the room is filled with light.

"Go on in," she reassured me.

A little girl is looking out the large glass window. She is small, her dark hair sweeps up on her soft pink cheek. Her profile is etched against the horizon. Her palm is on the window, her breath makes soft moist circles on the glass. She waits and watches.

"Who is she?" My therapist's voice was warm.

If she doesn't move, if she just stays right here, Solvig will return. I will not move, I will be good, and oh so still; and Solvig, my Solvig will find me.

My eyes opened suddenly. What was unearthed here? What was forgotten and split off from me? I recognized myself, but my mind did not comprehend. The facts were well known; I lived in Sweden for three years with a foster family, Solvig and Torsten. My mother returned and I left, she told me, *without once looking back.* My mind rushed up and swirled.

Lonely and solemn, little Tina has not moved from her place. "If you get lost," she was surely told, "stay where you are—we will find you." Patient and quiet, she waits for Solvig. She waits for me. Guardian of secrets and memories; my shadow—the real image the body creates in front or behind oneself.

Here was the heart of loss. To my three-year-old self, my foster family was *my* family. The day my mother rang Solvig's doorbell and brought me home as an adopted child, I lost my first mother and father, my three brothers, a home, a country, and a language. I lost myself and became another child. The shining child waited at the window. The dark child emerged. To the passing eye, I was unremarkable, even normal—but my inner self was silent, dark, and eternally sad for a loss that had no name.

That day in the therapist's office was the first in a decade of self-discovery. With her loving help, I pieced my childhood and myself back together. I collected fleeting images, dreams, and snatches of conversations, and created my own crazy quilt of my early life with remnants, embroidery, and bits of ribbon.

The path of memory was littered with startling beliefs and perceptions that operated, silent and deadly, behind the scenes. My progress was uneven. I reworked an understanding, leaped ahead, then wallowed for weeks in a fog. After a remission, I emerged to work on a new piece of the puzzle. The darkness began to lighten, my rage abated, my depressions lessened; I began to breathe.

Chapter 1

GRIEF'S GRACE

Solvig holds my arm as we turn to the camera. It is 1954, and we sit on a wooden bench, our feet tucked in the sand of the beach at Malmö. My two-year-old face is thrown back, my short black hair swept by the wind. I am relaxed in a smile.

The photo is a surprise. Thirty years later I study it carefully for the first time. A fingerprint smudges the edge. Solvig is movie-star slender and stylish in her sunglasses and short curly blond hair. We are dressed in white blouses and colorful skirts. She has me firmly at the elbow; her grasp is loving and protective. She keeps this child from flight.

༺☙༻

I was on the phone with an international operator. In 1986, I was suddenly possessed to find my foster family, the Elmståhls, whom I lived with in Sweden. I had been nestled deep there, adored as the only girl with three older brothers, Sven-Johan, Ulf, and my almost twin, Kjell-Olof. But I have not seen them or heard from them in over thirty years.

I braced myself in the corner of the kitchen and looked out into the side yard. February left the earth hard and bare in Philadelphia. The old crab tree's large trunk was wet with snow.

My mother had no idea how to find my foster mother. "Solvig and I stopped writing each other years ago," she exclaimed, exasperated. "Why don't you call the international operator and ask for her phone number?"

It was like a bolt of lightning. I trembled. For days I hesitated, pulling my courage together.

The operator was kind. "Sorry, there are no Elmståhls in the Malmö area." A keyboard clicked faintly. "I can check in the southern region of Sweden," she added helpfully. "Yes, there is a Sölve Elmståhl in Lund. Perhaps he will give you information."

I dialed his number and waited for the phone to switch over to an international call. The tone changed to the old-fashioned ring. A man answered. It was that simple.

"Hello, this is Tina. Tina Davidson from the US. I used to live with your family," I breathlessly guessed.

"Of course." His warm voice poured out of the phone. "They always told so many stories about you."

He was Sölve, the fourth son, born less than a year after I left. Solvig had been so distressed at my departure that she decided to have another child immediately. He filled me in on the rest of the family.

"And Solvig?"

"She died of pulmonary carcinoma less than a year ago."

My legs buckled; I slid down the cabinets to the floor. She smoked heavily, became ill, and stopped talking. Eleven months ago.

I sat on the floor for a long time after the call was finished, tears soaking my face. I hadn't realized the depth of my desire to hear her voice, feel the touch of her hands. But she had not waited for me.

Thirty years without her, and this narrow miss. This ever-so-slight beyond my grasp was eons of time. No sooner was my journey to find her begun than the door closed. She, my first mother, was lost again, irrevocably. What remained was grief.

Grief waited for me, patient and enduring, lurking behind my eyelids, coloring my life gray. The grief I did not know, hidden underneath the bed, stuffed in the back of the closet, locked behind closed doors, now emerged. I began to remember.

Like a hundred years of rain, grief poured, thrashed, and flooded; cascaded, thundered, then drizzled for months. Finally, there was a calm day between downpours. Still steamy and moist, the sky was colorless behind the clouds. My lungs filled with air for a moment.

Then more rain, washing in like a sudden storm; my body ached. Soon, however, another lull, a break in the weather. The sun is pale at the horizon.

Grief's grace, like a dewy mist, is the soft smell of spring returned.

Chapter 2

MORNINGS

Philadelphia (1986–1987)

"One must aspire to be a slave to sound."
Lionel Nowak[1]

March 1

The day is spent absorbed in composing. I sit here in my studio and look out the tall window on the old magnolia tree, whose double trunks twist around each other. The bark is gray and smooth. Flowers bob in the breeze. The dog's nails tap on the floor. She settles down with a long sigh.

My work has taken on a personality I didn't expect. The music moves from dissonance and distance through hypnotic ripping of chords and becomes more tonal, until finally the melodies come sweet and strong. I am uneasy about the transition, but let it be.

This month has been calm and certain, but as the composing winds down I become sad. At night I lie in bed next to Wood, wide-eyed under the skylight. Our daughter Cassie's breathing is audible from her bedroom. I had a haunting dream last night.

March 12

The end of the piece is in my ears. The ascending patterns reach above themselves, blindly searching with closed eyes and bare fingers. A complete calmness. The beginning empties up into the light, with more and more emotion.

But, I feel so much anger. I want to write this *Clear Piece*, but I cannot. My rage, the wrenching away, the intensity of not understanding my life keeps me from moving forward.

Am I a fragmented person, incapable of putting together a long, unified piece of music? If I open myself up to the joy and love that is there behind all those tears, will I be able to do more than one large ensemble scream?

My music becomes more and more tonal. I pause. My dissonance has protected me. Will I take such a risk and move into a tonal direction?

March 15

Yesterday we went with a friend to the Arboretum. The gray woods were beautiful against a gray sky, these slender distinctions. As we walked, I spoke about Sweden. Cassie picked up stones, holding them close to her chest in her chubby eighteen-month-old fingers. A small human magpie.

April 1

The shape of the piece becomes clear. There are options for open orchestration with an improvised section moving into rhythms, and finally a return to the chords. A bitterness creeps back in; its insistence is loud—a flash and then a calming down. A Swedish melody emerges like a ray of light. It is slowly reabsorbed into the fabric of the soft, undulating chords.

April 3

What kind of sense does this all make? Why is it clear? What is the flash? A return to chords?

April 15

Night sweats. I am back in my childhood years in Istanbul. An idea for a new piece emerges; back to that room up beyond the stairs (those terrible secrets).

April 25

Requiem for Something Lost came out like a tubercular blood clot for saxophone quartet and prerecorded tape of rustling whispers. As I wrote, I worried it was too strong, too revealing.

The new path I have been searching for these last months stands before me. I was looking for a difference, a change—more joy and love. But what I find is me. Right here, I find myself.

I need not to compose about sorrow or grief but about my life, my history, my legacy. When I reveal myself, I speak for others.

What happened? I bumped into something and realized it was myself.

July 7

I have completed a lullaby, a piece that invites dreams and sleep as opposed to hard conscious thought. It is my song for Solvig. She would have sung this to me, her fingers interwoven in my three-year-old hand. For you to sing to me.

July 12
Wood's surgical residency at Temple University begins. He is out of the house almost continually. The transition from a two-parent household to one is enormous. I wrestle with running a household, schedules, and childcare. Frustration leaks out, but slowly I learn to care for Cassie and myself.

July 20
Descending Figure for voice and open instrumentation is begun. The piece is a setting of three poems by Louise Glück, who describes the death of her little sister long ago. It is, Glück claims, "wrong, wrong/to hold her—/Let her be alone/without memory."[2]

No. Stop. I am enraged and cannot agree. I will hold you in my arms, rock you. Listen to the hum of my voice through my body. Listen to my breath filling my lungs, to the distant thump of my heart.

July 22
I want to put my finger on the grief unending. I want the audience to be unable to break away. Why "descending figure"?

August 5
I have a sharp memory from my childhood. Alone in a crib, I throw my head back and howl. I hit my head against the bars; I shake them. It is a memory from my years in Sweden. I cannot grasp it.

September 2
Labor Day is gone; summer is over. This morning, I lie in bed with my daughter, snuggled in. "Hug me," she commands. We breathe together.

I am floating again, these past few days. I must be about to come to some new knowledge, or perhaps I already have but have not accepted it. I'm not sure, so I float and can't remember.

September 5
A few days up at the Charles Ives Center for the Performing Arts gives me relief. I am in residence with musician, composer, and maverick Pauline Oliveros. "Hear, remember, and imagine," she intones. You hear a sound, remember it, and then imagine it again. She uses words to form her music, bringing the performers into the process of creation. Her work begets community.

I am struck by music's linear process, where duration is the great ingredient. Unlike visual art, music cannot be experienced all at once. Instead it moves through time. As we listen, we construct the whole in our mind through memory. Like a transparent ghost, music moves our hearts with its lack of tangible substance.

My life, like my music, has a similar flow—the present is made whole by memory. I stumble often, however, with so many gaps and misunderstandings.

September 17
My piece has finally become *Descending Figure with Lullaby*. After finishing the three-set, I added the lullaby I wrote the month before. While Glück's poems rage at the loss of a child, the lullaby reclaims. Love, wordless love, ultimately is the only answer. *Lullaby* rests well.

September 26
Today I tried on dresses to be married in. I am filled with unexpected joy. After seven years of living together, Wood and I will make it official in November.

September 29
The darkness of candles in the corner. Dim lighting, the lighting of truths. My sister Eva's poem "Shadow Grief" haunts me:

> *In my own way,*
> *I still light a candle*
> *For that child*
> *And call her by name.*[3]

What is it I fear? That if I light a candle and call myself by name, there will be no response?

My early childhood was like the desolation after a holocaust. No God could exist. It was deep darkness. This desolation has been the only concrete piece of evidence I had that I was still alive. I clutch onto it. Can I risk letting it go? And what if there is nothing behind it? I will have less than I have now—a void is worse than destruction and ruins. Do I risk the little I have for nothing?

September 30
Never Love a Wild Thing for open instrumentation was well received at the concert. The work has a vitality and wonder to it. I panicked before the performance, but the music is strong and clear, a reflection of a growing inner energy.

October 5

A dream haunts me. I close my eyes and am caught in the ruined walls of the house. I reach out to touch the surface. How light and airy the house once was! A black Steinway piano stood next to white walls, which reached up for stories. The wind gently brushed the curtains of the open windows. Calm, white, the green of outside.

I could have been happy here; this could have been home. Now it is damaged beyond repair. My eyes linger over the lost promise. The walls are blackened and yet cool. Rooms are empty, lath sticks through the plaster, floors creak. The roof is open to the sky. A great sadness, a sigh suspends my body. My mind fingers this dream as one would an old plaything. A touch awakens memories.

Who is this man? He knows the little girl. He shuts the door to the dead one. He and I escape together. He hands me an infant.

October 7

Such anger these days. Why am I not satisfied with the gains I have made in my work? I feel awake to an old hunger to be more visible.

Last night Wood put Cassie in her bed. She cried out and rushed back to us. "I need kisses!"

"Of course you do," he replied, gently picking her up and carrying her back to bed.

October 10

I have begun a new piece for solo voice and prerecorded voices. The music is melodic. My palms itch when I sing it, as if the melodies were coming out of my flesh.

21

October 11

My anger has made me stiff and tall. I walk rigidly down the road. Do I really know where I am going? If there is no anger, who am I? It gets me up in the morning, keeps my spine straight, pushes me into my work. It guards over me and keeps the hurtful ones away.

"Will you leave me?" I am naked and scared.

"No, I will not leave you. We will do this together."

"But, where am I going?" Anger has always chosen the path.

"I don't know. Our movements will be slow, we will move carefully. Wait."

October 12

Who is that voice, this other? Who is she? She is not one of the little ones, but large and encompassing. Smiling when one of the others has a tantrum, she is tolerant and knowing. "This is as it should be." She watches without interfering.

Large and distant like the sky. Limitless, loving, and compassionate. She encompasses and surrounds. Balanced and focused, her toes feel the earth like roots feel the soil. When she touches the sky, she is part of it. She knows how to wait and be patient, knows her own body because she has listened. Her senses are acute because she trusts. Never uncomfortable or dispassionate. She does not see into the future or pretend she can. She knows truth as freedom and ease.

I blush. It is vain and arrogant to acknowledge her existence. I avert my eyes. My awake self does not trust she is part of me.

October 17

I dreamed all night about the woman with silver hair.

October 20
I am testing the difference between knowing and knowledge. Knowledge is a noun, knowing is a verb. Knowledge is permanence, an arrival to a destination, a measure of power, and a method of control; it is a command, and a grasp with expertness or skill. Knowing, on the other hand, is to perceive, sense, or see; it is to trust and listen, to hear and accept things beyond one's imagination. Knowing is not being able to explain, but being able to expand and grow continuously. Unfixed and inexhaustible. Knowing is to be.

What is this sudden fear? If knowing is to recognize oneself, why this debate, this holding back? My stomach clenches; the risk of seeing all of me overwhelms. Can I dare to go forward? After a lifetime of less, the possibility of more is terrifying.

October 22
A member of the board of directors for our new music ensemble sits next to me at the concert. He is handsome, with curly gray hair and a young tan face. I've always liked him.

We listen to Sussan Deyhim improvise, her dark Iranian voice is powerful and rich. She is a sorceress, a spinner, and weaves her performance art in arcs around us. Don whispers to me, "I bet she's a bitch to live with." For a moment I can't take it in. The fear of women with power, of women with truth and knowing, is palpable.

November 6
Nothing. Absolutely nothing. I have nothing to say. I am stationary.

November 11
Still nothing. Silence. I sort out my desk, doing paperwork all morning. My dreams are vague and hard to remember. They fade quickly. Waiting for the music is disquieting.

November 13
I am suddenly surging ahead. I was always here but didn't recognize it. I see again the bridge and hear the rumble, the savage dance, the callbacks, the change, and finally clarity. The echoes are both of the past and the future. We pass on to the promised land; chords cascade quietly. The arrival, a place of stillness and clearness.

November 24
The day is beautiful with a cold sun in blue-gray skies for a wedding. I spend a quiet time dressing in my soft silk dress with my two sisters. Midmorning, Wood and I stand on the porch, the minister between us, friends and family ringed around us. The ceremony is brief, and as we speak our vows the clock chimes. Cassie wriggles down from my brother's grasp and runs up to us. Jumping into my arms, she cries, "I hear de clock. I hear de clock."

We laugh and cry. We are married.

December 5
Eva's apartment is sparsely furnished with Amish quilts and family memorabilia hanging on the walls, spotless and mute.

I love rooms that wait for you to pour in warmth and presence. Her rooms are cool, as if they were icons—one side of the face is revealed as they gaze off, away from you. In the corner, a tall case holds swatches of neatly stacked material. I finger the colors and textures of her silk and rayon fabric. On the top shelf are bottles of buttons, brilliant jewels. Plants sit on a glass shelf, glistening.

Eva pours her warmth into her poems these days; I pour mine into music.

December 6
Shining Child. Dark Child. My daughter helps me remember both.

The shining child is the outside curve of my face and body. The top layer of my skin has hardened and cracked off, pushing forward in shining fanatic love and awe. Thin and luminescent, she has little substance, a child of the shade. She blends in, disappears into the fabric.

The dark child is cloaked and mute, curled over sorrow like an oyster over a grain of sand. He lurks on the edge of rage.

Is the shining child only a paper facade, an unreal manifestation of the dark one—the real child? Does the shining child participate in love?

December 7
Where does the dark child live?

December 8
My mother's voice is upbeat. "I can't believe how cheerful you are about your heart condition!"

I quickly change the subject. I don't want to talk about these past several years of living with congestive heart failure, the careful planning of each day to balance rest and activity, the joint pain, the intermittent coughing, or the exhaustion. I worry that my condition will worsen, and I will leave Cassie without a mother. Death, always a friend, is now a feared enemy.

What do I say to the quivering child inside me? I am fragile. I feel Solvig's death and my own darkness. As joy becomes possibility, I look into the sky with new sharpness. When I die, will I become the sky? Where or when was never an issue to a child already dead inside. Living has taken on a measure of terror.

December 17

I wake hearing the piece I am struggling over. It is like the thrill of first being in love—to wake dreaming of the new work. The music comes from deep inside, resonating with the outside world.

Sound is all around me. My denim skirt swishes between my legs when I walk fast and hard. I laugh and almost jump with pleasure. It is the whip of sails against the mast, it is the sound of laundry being hung out on a cold day, of curtains in a heavy, dusty breeze.

Did Solvig snap her sheets on cold afternoons? My muscles pull in a fast walk, my legs scissor, my breath intake is sharp. A feeling of invigoration floods me, warm muscles well used. Cold cheeks.

Levin, in the Russian novel *Anna Karenina,* works with the peasants mowing the grass by hand. Taking up the long scythe, he cuts row after row, his muscles sliding smoothly over each other, emitting heat. As he mows he becomes the scythe, the grass, and the work itself. Exhausted, he rests with the others eating lunch, and again to work, all afternoon into the early evening. And then, as exhaustion is about to break him, annihilate him, he falls asleep. When he wakes, he looks about him. "I am! I feel!" All is new.

December 15
I feel Solvig's hand on my shoulder these days. Her love helps me accept my unreasonable departure from her life. Her warmth allows me to turn more toward the west, toward Terry, my mother. Perhaps I can take Terry's hand, hold it, and explore. Between worlds, between families, between grief.

December 28
I look back at the long horizontal arc of my childhood. I see nothing for the first three years in Sweden. Then there is light and a great separation. The shining child goes forward, overwhelmed by a powerful white brilliance; the dark child stays behind.

The three years of living abroad in Istanbul are the most balanced and colorful time of my young years. But by my sister's second birthday and our return to the US, I begin the long, narrow descent into darkness. The elementary school years in central New York are cloudy and gray. High school is pitch black. In college, there are long blank patches of time that I simply do not remember.

I used to dream that I was slowly drowning in quicksand, sinking despite every effort to free myself. How did I survive?

Chapter 3

FAMILY PHOTO

I am flying. Down the sharp incline of the backyard, I skim the grass, jettisoning off rocks. The creek below shimmers. Pausing on the rusting rail of the metal staircase, I listen. The world hums, the sounds cascading around me. I jump into the air like Peter Pan, fly down the long staircase and over the creek. I dive into the water, a sleek little girl, a seal pup. Suddenly, I am drowning. I cannot breathe.

❧

None of us are sure whether my mother was in love with my stepfather when they married. The courtship was difficult and unsure; my mother's heart had been given away and broken long before. But my stepfather was handsome, virile, and pursued her relentlessly.

I was four when they met. My mother had brought me from Sweden in 1956, and we settled in Athens, Ohio, where she had a teaching position in the English department. This was her first job after receiving a PhD and a fresh start. She filled our large dark house with furniture and rented rooms to female students. My favorite was Clela, who dressed me as a princess in her soft slips, painting my lips dark and pulling up my hair with jewelry.

My stepfather was still writing his dissertation when he ended up teaching alongside my mother. I imagine that he saw her across the room at a faculty meeting or bumped into her in the hall. He introduced himself at a cocktail party. They stood, leaning slightly on the back of a couch, in conversation. Abruptly he turned and walked away without a word.

"What a strange man," my mother murmured. When he later asked her out for dinner, he was already set in his desire to marry her.

Loren Kenneth Davidson came from a colorful background steeped in the dark passion of religious fundamentalism. His great-great-grandfather fought in the Revolutionary War, and his grandfather was gored to death by a bull. His father, Harrison, became a preacher in rural Pennsylvania with five children.

Soon my stepfather's family life was eclipsed when Zelda, the blond curly-haired four-year-old, suddenly died. His mother went to bed—for how long, no one can remember. But one morning she arose and took her place in the kitchen. She had a dream, a vision. Jesus appeared and hovered at the foot of her bed. "You are saved," He said. "You are saved. You are *saved!*"

With frightening zeal the family became born-again Christians. While his siblings became missionaries and preachers, my stepfather stayed apart. He went to Scotland to study and did his graduate work at Duke University. Always up for an adventure, he and a friend constructed a raft and floated down the Mississippi River looking for Mark Twain. When his brother stopped writing his family while converting the nomads in Africa, my stepfather was sent to find him. Together they rode halfway across the Sahara Desert on camel before my stepfather became ill and they turned back.

Trece to her family and Terry to her friends, my mother was the third child of four. Her mother, Edith, a tiny slender woman whose family escaped the Irish potato famine, was passionate about progressive education for children. Her father, handsome John (Jack) Aney, received his college degree from Syracuse University and worked as a military demolition expert.

My mother lived a protected, light-filled childhood. The family fortune disappeared during the Great Depression, yet they lived a modest upper-middle-class lifestyle. She was adored by her father, who inspired her to reach high. She graduated in 1944 from State University of New York, formerly New York State College for Teachers.

My mother was worldly, smart, and articulate. She was a WAC (Women's Army Corps) during World War II and decoded Japanese secret messages. One of the few women in higher education at that time, she got a doctorate in comparative literature from the University of Pennsylvania in the 1950s, played the violin, and spoke several languages. She had East Coast breeding and liberal sensibilities. And she matched my stepfather's sense of adventure; she loved to travel and learn new things.

I hold these early days of their marriage in the bright part of my memory. I see them sway back and forth to the rhythm of their courtship. I remember when they enjoyed each other, laughing with friends over dinner, talking animatedly about literature and philosophy in the kitchen.

But he was gruff with me and often silent; his large hand enveloped mine. His blue eyes were rarely warm.

One cool evening, the three of us had been out late. I drowsed on the drive home; the car filled with the hum of voices, my parents' faces illuminated by the drifting glare of oncoming headlights. My mother went ahead to unlock the front door while my stepfather stooped and picked me up from the back seat. I lay half asleep against his chest, for a moment comfortable. Then, looking up at his large face, I reached up and pinched the soft folds under his chin. His breath caught, but he said nothing. I dug in my nails and pinched again and again as he carried me into the house.

That Christmas we drove down to Key West. They decided to marry without informing their families. I had just turned five and was excited about the word "elope." I knelt, solemnly saying amen in my odd, slightly Swedish accent alongside two elderly witnesses. The priest's voice echoed in the empty church.

They were newlyweds with a plan: to publish a book of interviews of famous living authors. And who, in 1957, would they start with but the old man himself, the greatest living American author—Ernest Hemingway.

We wandered around in Key West. They took photographs of the sprawling Hemingway House and went to his favorite hangout, Sloppy Joe's Bar. But the weather turned cold, and we shivered in our jackets. Why not fly south to Cuba, my parents reasoned, and find his home in a grove of trees? How they got the nerve, I have no idea—a charming sense of bravura or, as young professionals, their idealism overcame any second thoughts.

We arrived in Havana on a warm, beautiful Christmas Eve. By evening, my parents managed to get Hemingway's phone number and address. Hesitantly, my stepfather placed the call. Much to his surprise, "Papa" answered the phone and grumpily suggested they come by the next morning.

Hemingway lived ten miles from Havana, in the village of San Francisco de Paula on a plantation he called *Finca Vigía* (Lookout Farm). It was a large limestone villa surrounded by acres of banana trees, tropical shrubs, and gardens. We trudged up the long driveway to his house.

Hemingway was immediately not pleased. Seeing my step-father's camera, he suspected my parents of being journalists and not young college teachers as they claimed. Moreover, he had to fix his oven to roast his Christmas turkey for guests that evening.

"Oh," my mother said, "why don't you let my husband help?"

"Humph," said Hemingway, still seething, "I'd rather not have my turkey."

Only later did Hemingway grudgingly let my stepfather take photos of him, beautiful in his white beard and long blue shirt covering his belly. The sun was high overhead, the garden dark green. Four years later he would die at his own hands one morning, shooting himself with a double-barreled shotgun.

I sat on my mother's lap. Etched in my memory is the large wrought-iron fence that surrounded his house, his dark study, and a man whose face I could not quite see.

Over the next few years, my parents interviewed dozens of authors. They wrote and received invitations from James Thurber, Norman Mailer, Muriel Rukeyser, Pearl Buck, Thornton Wilder, William Carlos Williams, May Swenson, Catherine Drinker Bowen, and John Ciardi, to name a few. Katherine Ann Porter was lovely and charming; Carson McCullers was dying; James

Baldwin came to a party in his honor at my parent's home. After his interview, Carl Sandburg found me curled up asleep in his easy chair. I was sucking my thumb. "See how I affect the young ladies these days," he laughed.

On the trip back home from their wedding in Florida, my parents decided to visit my stepfather's parents. My mother had not met them previously. The drive up to Kentucky was long, and we arrived exhausted at the trim white family home in Wilmore late at night. My stepfather's mother met us at the door in a thin cotton bathrobe and invited us in. The kitchen table was quickly covered with food. We held hands while grace was said.

Grandmother wasted no time in sizing up her new daughter-in-law. She demanded to know if she drank, or perhaps smoked, and if she had accepted Jesus as her personal savior. The answers did not meet with her satisfaction; the visit was long.

Just before we left, we gathered for a family photo. Grandmother is calm, her battleship jaw jutting out. Gladys, her adopted daughter, rests a slender arm on her shoulder. My grandfather, in his Sunday best, is jug-eared and stern. My mother, her high collared wool suit neatly hugging her, smiles brightly. Uncle Harrison scowls, his thin bow tie slightly off center. The family has come to an uneasy truce in regard to my parents' marriage.

I, on the other hand, held a different opinion. My five-year-old face contorts in comedic social commentary. I leer, I grimace, my eyes shine.

We begin our family journey.

Chapter 4

WINTER

Philadelphia (1988)

Women have been Cassandras all along—pointing out the fault lines due to slippage and warning the other sex of the damage we are doing to our planet and our own future as a species.

Erica Jong[1]

January 4

A new year. I am full of optimism. I write my orchestra piece with a sigh of homecoming. The music is clear and shimmering. When I compose, I enter a focused state where time and life's problems have no meaning. I wake to the real world for a few minutes, do some tasks, then quickly duck back in.

February 1

At bedtime, Cassie is in tears. She stands in the hallway, her three-year-old shoulders drooping. "I miss Anne," she wails. Her nursery teacher left a few months ago. I promise to ease my work schedule and play with her tomorrow at school. I will stay until story time.

An illogical fear that the upcoming premiere of *Descending Figure with Lullaby* will result in some undefined loss overwhelms me. Revealing my own childhood in my music is frightening. But there is the *Lullaby*. Solvig wraps her arms tightly around me and sings.

37

February 4

After all my anxiety and procrastination, the last half of the orchestra piece quickly falls into place. I finish for the day and wonder what will come next. The melodies soar, still with a tinge of sadness. The opening is a growth, with rumbles of birth and heaving of layers of earth. The timpani is semi-pitched (semi-human, semi-focused), a dark noise of my growing life force. Energy and heat, and then a radiance—long solo lines for strings, a step inside the fire.

Sweden looms large these days. I have scheduled a concert tour of my music in Amsterdam, Belgium, and Sweden. I will take Cassie; she is now the same age as I was when I left Sweden, a vibrant, talkative three-year-old.

February 15

It comes back to me. In my insecurity, I rush from myself, snatching melodies away too soon. I reveal my deepest feelings but only in brief exposures. One day I hope to find ease and even gait in my music. The work on this orchestra piece is calm, even, and flushed. I find new footholds; the work goes on.

February 23

The day is warm and sunny; the first purple crocus peeks out of the damp autumn leaves. Joy is sudden, then quickly sorrow. When the earth burgeons, I feel a depth of darkness. I miss Solvig the most when the flowers are tossed in cool wind and the sun is warm on my legs. I smell Istanbul, the dark blue Bosphorus, and the tiny flowers on the plateau. I walk the field above my stepfather's farm; the daffodils are not yet bloomed.

February 29
Leap day of the leap year and Wood's last day of work at this hospital. He takes a big yellow bag with him to pack his books, papers, and hospital coats. He leaves this part of his life behind, unfinished.

Last night we lay in bed angry. Finally he said, "You are upset because I am no longer pursuing a career as a surgeon."

I sink into the pillows. Today it is quiet between us, a hiatus.

March 1
Cassie dances in the living room at night. She stands quietly for a moment, listening to the music, and then moves each shoulder slightly, turns in circles, and lifts up her skirt. Swaying and rotating around the rug, she is introspective, beautiful, and undeniably sensual. A solemn child dancing for herself.

March 8
I am absorbed in the premiere performance of *Descending Figure with Lullaby*. The soprano has had every problem imaginable with the piece, and the rehearsals have sagged. Finally, at the dress rehearsal, there is a promise of crystallization. But during the performance a ground wire loosens in the speaker, a cold wind on stage tosses music around, and the large loading dock door rattles. The piece disintegrates, the audience hesitates before applauding. I close my ears to any of the praise and watch for lack of eye contact.

April 13
The preparation for a European tour of my music continues; Cassie and I leave soon. Many good things are happening quickly.

The orchestra piece is progressing at its own pace. *Transparent Victims* was selected to represent the USA in the International Rostrum of Composers. The famous Kronos Quartet called to talk about commissioning a new piece from me. I am thrilled and terrified.

April 22

The concert in Belgium goes well. I play several of my piano pieces and give a lecture about my larger works.

My stepfather accompanies Cassie and me on the tour. He is in a world of abstraction and is more reserved and private than usual. He sits hours next to me while traveling, silent and dark. When we arrive at a hotel or go eat, he suddenly springs to life, smiles at the hostess, leans to one side, and regales the waiter with off-color jokes.

April 24

We spend a long and cold day on an excursion down the Rhine, then take the overnight train to Copenhagen. I am tense and irritable. By evening, in a private home, an hour on the playground, and a meal of cold meat and cheese, I am in better spirits. I soak long in a deep white tub.

April 26

The final concert is in Stockholm tonight, and we go to Gislaved tomorrow. I am without any thoughts. We will stay with the Elmståhls, my foster family. Thirty years ago I was Cassie's age. Thirty years ago Solvig held me and laughed with me.

April 29

My foster brother Kjell-Olof is tall, thin, and boyish. He talks while unloading our luggage from the train. Like most Swedes, his English is excellent, and he points out the dark Swedish woods and elk crossings as we drive. Sitting cross-legged on the long couch in his living room, he smokes constantly. Black-and-white photographs pile on the coffee table, each with a story about Solvig and our life together. She played the harmonica. She smoked small cigars. Kjell-Olof and I grew up together like twins. We slept side by side, ate together. We were constant companions.

"Even though I was a few months older," he muses in his singsong accent, "you always led the way."

We visit Torsten, my foster father, in his small home. The entire family gathers for a Swedish luncheon, and we eat all afternoon long: *sill* (herring) and sour cream, small new potatoes with dill, and delicious crisp bread. All four boys and their families laugh and talk over each other, their Swedish words like kayaks bouncing down a rushing rapid. Torsten's face glows with the light of his family.

Sven-Johan's wife hands me a small box. "Solvig gave these when we had our daughter. She had saved them all these years." Inside, wrapped in tissue papers, are two tiny little dresses—Tina's baby clothes. My baby clothes.

Solvig had not expected my mother to return for me after she was away for three years. I had been with the Elmståhls long enough that they no longer thought of me (or I them) as anything but family.

I do not know of her heartbreak, only of mine. Solvig quietly let me go and kept these small dresses. I bring them to my face and breathe them in.

June 14

We have returned to Philadelphia. My health, with the sudden heat, is precarious. Yesterday I rushed to the doctor with weakness and an irregular heartbeat. I waited, not knowing if this was a passing unevenness or a decline.

Seven years ago I said goodbye to a Tina whose everlasting good health had no end and gradually accepted the Tina with congestive heart failure. A routine visit to the dentist, perhaps a slip of the hand, and I became infected with bacteria that lodged in my heart, eating holes in the mitral valve leaflets. My heart pumps but cannot seal off the blood flow, which returns to my lungs and weakens them. I wake tired, my joints ache; I have a persistent cough.

Since my illness, I have readjusted everything: shortened my working hours, given up performing, focused on composing, and rested during the day.

The years have been long and full, as if time slowed. I have thrived. But I forgot that my heart has its own life span that dictates mine. Am I now moving down to a slower level of activity?

I hate this.

June 15

I had a long, good cry yesterday.

August 19

The four-cello piece is coming quickly and quietly—*Dark Child Sings*, the dark child in me. She sings of the coming of age, of growing love and vibrancy, and the strength and flexibility of the inner voice. The opening section is woody, sensuous, and ever ascending. The music fills my ears.

42

August 20

Our house in Philadelphia is in the middle of renovations. I hired my brother Scott and his friend. They are loud; they shout and jostle each other with exuberance. The house fills with dust as they tear down the lath and plaster. Equipment litters the floor. They pause, their tool belts slung low on their hips. Sweat drips off their arms.

I write music through the noise and listen to them, smiling. Their male energy hums through the house. At night, strange dreams haunt me. Images are indistinct, and faces swirl around when I wake. I feel their dewy dampness.

August 21

Cassie and I have escaped to the shore at the family home in Mantoloking, New Jersey. Here I can rest, recover my health. I can clean out my head, change my pace, slow down, and let the string piece for the Kronos Quartet rise to the surface. The music needs space.

The weather is suddenly cool, with brilliant blue skies, warm sun, and a quiet breeze. Clear skinned, Cassie sleeps on the porch. She will wake soon. "Mother," she will call. "Mother! Come here!" —more like "mo-thar."

Why am I now restless without a schedule? Remove the discipline from my life, and I am nervous and fussy.

My music does not always allow me to be with myself. Without music, I am plain and unremarkable. I shop, eat, dally about, think foolish thoughts, peer into the mirror. I hate, I love, I sleep, I anguish—nothing special. But when focused on writing music, I am a channel, a beam of light—I am a passageway for what must come out. My entire person comes together in a pulse, condensed and absorbed. The work follows me everywhere. I hear it in the bathroom, while I am cooking, as I fall asleep. There is always this murmur, this whisper.

August 23
I scrub the kitchen floor and think of the Shakers' motto "Hands to work, hearts to God." For them, every part of life is a spiritual manifestation of God—the God within—whether they make furniture or say their prayers. Cleaning the floor is a reflection of our lives. We keep our place of rest with care and openness; it is evidence of the way we live.

Hands to Work, Hearts to God. Everything is us; every part is a reflection of the inner light. The house we live in is also the house within. As my home becomes open for others, warm and comfortable, my soul becomes receptive and alive.

I strip the mantelpiece in the living room of the old varnish and paint spots. I work carefully so the solvents don't burn my skin or fall on the floor. The wood gleams softly at me, long hidden under dark, cracked varnish.

August 30
I have been slowly guiding my thoughts of the new piece for the Kronos Quartet, *Cassandra Sings*. My health has rallied, and I am full of careful energy.

Singing is deeply personal. The warm breath from within flows over the vocal cords—moisture from the seat of the soul. In the Greek play *Agamemnon* by Aeschylus, Cassandra sings her lines, as she must, for she, like the chorus, speaks the truth. As Richard Lattimore says in the introduction to his translation, she sings the reality of life "not only past and future, but present, what is occurring right now beyond that fragmentary point of space where she stands."[2]

Singing Magic.

Cassandra is a meeting point of all dimensions of time. She, like truth, is the point where all can be seen at once. Past, present, and future; a trinity of views. An all-seeing eye, she is an egoless function of life and a resource unused.

In my mind, the mythological Cassandra is wonderfully adolescent, energetic, and young. The underground temple is dark, and the initiation ritual for young priestesses begins. She consecrates her slim body, energy, and sexual being to the larger whole. She gives herself over and offers heart and body to God.

My string quartet is both about the Cassandra of myth and about me. Initiated into a spiritual world, where the dreams are alive, we are consumed with the pain of living. The truth is stunning and possessing. We shriek, howl, and, in the midst, we die. At the same moment we are born into a continuity, a joy. Awake, we are flowing and skimming.

The tragedy of Cassandra of old is that no one believed her vision. But is that not always the case? Either words are inarticulate, too softly spoken or loudly shouted, or we simply are not ready, not able to hear. The ensuing silence creates a void where we are reduced, mocked, and murdered.

But Cassandra of the present, my daughter, Cassie, sings to me. Cassandra of old. Tina of the present. Cassie of the future.

September 1

Bruce Chatwin, in his book *The Songlines,* suggests that the

Aboriginals sing the world into existence. Songs, or "dreaming," are a primitive map of the world. Their natural soul describes the country in its most primary form.

My music springs from an idea first formulated in words. The titles come well before the music itself and are, to some extent, my map of the world, guiding me as I compose. They are metaphors or secret encoded meanings for my pieces that I understand, do not understand, and come to understand. *Dark Child Sings*, for example, is my dark child singing out his life, with growing ecstasy and passion, of sexual beginnings, of calm lullabies, and of strong chants.

I have a love affair with the poetry of words. Strung together, they are both important and not, mysterious and clear. Occasionally, words stand in the way of my music, speaking louder than the piece itself, because I simply do not know yet. I cannot dig beyond the phrase.

Music is never just passion or reason, instead a delicate balance between opposites that need the other to exist. Without one there are neither. Reason, brittle and devoid of passion, can be a monster of blindness and self-service. And passion without reason is bloated and ridiculous.

September 15

This morning I remembered a faint glimmering of a ruined house in last night's dream. Nostalgia swirls up and brings tears. The sadness is worn, soft like an old sweater.

How is it that I am present one moment, then in the past? I am constantly caught between worlds. I talk on the phone or cook dinner, and suddenly am displaced, walking into an overgrown garden. I scuff the path and breathe in the colors that dance in the sunlight. My feet skate on thin mud. I watch a small snake ripple out of my way. Then I push the memories back like window curtains and walk into the present.

September 16
Our Philadelphia home is slowly coming back from the renovations. Yesterday the floors were finished and the plastic was removed—a wonderful moment when the furniture is pushed back, rugs are replaced, the floors are clean and open again. As I set to work on the new string quartet, I feel my personal windows and hatches closing. I am going inside to work.

September 21
Yesterday was terrible. Fear. Panic. I got phone calls from friends asking about the string quartet. The *New York Times* announced the premiere scheduled in Alice Tully Hall today. David Harrington of Kronos Quartet called to see how things were going. I can't breathe. I can't think. I am just in the beginning stages of writing.

September 22
I am in labor pain with my piece. The contractions are strong and startling. Every time I feel that tightness rise, I have to sit down and breathe. The sound of my lungs, the rasp of air rushing in, calms and strengthens me.

    Cassandra Sings is about consolidation. The composing seems much less fragmentary, more unified than usual. Pain stabs her eyes, she cries in the heartbreak of human suffering. She gives herself to the spiritual life, an adolescent throbbing. The whirling of the dervishes, the acceptance of the snake of life biting her foot, and transformation into true oneness. She emerges like a swallow gliding out on a song. She comes out of dark waters like Venus, her skin radiant and white.

September 26
On Saturday morning I was a wreck. I wanted to run into my studio every minute and work, driving, driving, nervous pushing. I hold back.

October 3
A great day. I can hear. And I am dreaming again. The dreams are busy, as if they were leading my daily life for me while I concentrate on the symbol. My dreams wash dishes, tend the garden, and pay bills. I sleep well, though my stomach is still tender.

I came in and immediately worked out several sections, streamlining the shape of the piece, reducing it to two sections. I get to the point right away. The old sense of balance and confidence returns. The end of the piece is already written, and I am anxious to compose toward it.

Most difficult is to wait until my unconscious offers up the music to my conscious. A patient waiting, an eternal sense of trust, and then, suddenly, clarity.

October 9
The string quartet continues to fall into shape, and the work is exciting. The previous agony was pressure during the most vulnerable stages of composing, of gathering the raw material together, finding tiny bits of flesh, atoms, or protoplasm. The stuff of

creation is a delicate process, full of uncertainty and patience. It is a time when I am open to all the fears and outside pressures.

The first section is almost completely mapped out. The rhythm tears along, bumping into sounds that are both unexpected and comfortable. I spin through reams of material, yet it is all connected somehow; tense, pressured, chased, inescapable, and swept away. I stitch together the fabric of the piece carefully, paying great attention to the transitions. The directions surprise the ear and are somehow just right. The new shape of the piece pleases me and has released the music inside. Unbelievable.

October 12
I started to slip into panic yesterday, but caught myself.

November 2
Parenting brings me to the reality of life. I am undone by its difficulties. This morning after breakfast, Cassie is upset by a small thing. "Fix it!" she demands. I reach forward, both knowing that I can do nothing and hoping that I can. She snaps like a spring in a clock. The tantrum rages for almost an hour. I find myself picking her up to shake her out of it.

In moments like these, I stand outside myself. I am both the child possessed by the cyclone of feelings and the adult trying to stop the child from crying. The failure is a twofold loss of self, and the scream obliterates all. I surge up, out of my inabilities, to force both back into place. I am the emptiness of not having the self, and the clamping down of the iron fist. I shake her and, at the same time, am being shaken by my stepfather. We both fall into the chasm.

A memory of dusk and growing cold days comes to me—pressed in a crowd of people, ripe fruit almost within touch, and being utterly alone.

November 12

I am working on the last large section of *Cassandra Sings*. I am more relaxed. When I am half asleep I hear the running melodies like streams of water. They soothe me and allow me to sleep.

The other night, I saw Paula Sepinuck's choreography to my cello quartet, *Dark Child Sings*. It was beautiful, central, and rooted.

December 16

The year closes quickly. Composing music is a humbling experience, much like being a parent. Before conception there is an utter lack of understanding of what it is to be a parent, coupled with the terror of losing individuality. But within five minutes of holding one's child, the past life is irrevocably forgotten. All is transformed, and life without this being is inconceivable and obscene.

The work on the quartet has been a sickening roller-coaster ride. Writing the first section was like going through a manic depressive storm—at times ecstatic, at others agonizingly difficult. But then the second section rolls out easily. Already I am at Cassandra's true joy. My dreams are released. I fly along with my music.

Chapter 5

GARDEN OF EDEN

Wisteria winds around the front porch; the blossoms droop softly. Blue-purple petals litter the ground. A short walk through dark woods, the plateau bursts in a meadow full of tiny flowers; the grass ripples. The wind flutes in your ears and gravel crunches underfoot. And below, where the plateau meets the sky, is the blue, blue Bosphorus. The water is ice cold and flows out of the Black Sea to the Mediterranean. Some mornings, delicate white jellyfish inhale and exhale gracefully. Other mornings, schools of silvery sardines dart and zigzag. The Bosphorus, like the heart of my childhood, is dark, deep, and unfathomable.

༄

In truth, my parents were adventurers masquerading as literature professors. My mother was a particularly good teacher and fiercely dedicated to her students, but she, like my stepfather, loved to travel. After their first few years of marriage, we moved to Istanbul. I was six. My mother taught at the American College for Girls, and my stepfather at Roberts College. We lived on campus, in an apartment in the Turkish Sultan jeweler's former summer palace, a large, square, four-story building.

Turkey was a time of great awakenings. Bread was fragrant and hot out of large brick ovens; white cheese dripped with brine; yogurt was thick like heavy whipped cream; and rolls of apricot leather, sharp and tangy, were riddled with small stones I loved to dig out. In the evening, we walked through the main food market, illuminated by bare light bulbs. I lagged. The vendors called sharply. Fruits and vegetables were stacked and swollen with color, pungent fish, and the push of shoppers. My mother grabbed my hand.

The Turks have a special fondness for children. "Mashala," they'd laugh, pinch my cheeks red, and press fruit or candy in my hand. We were often at the campus dining hall. Mustapha, his white coat starched and stiff, always had a treat hidden in his pocket. He smiled as he revealed the apple, and I was fascinated by his long fingernail that curled delicately from his pinky.

My one true friend was David, who lived directly above us. His head was large and he moved with jerky motions; he was a faithful henchman. Spying on the college students from the woods, we played with the many feral cats and threw small green apples over the wall at Turkish workers, who patiently steered their laden donkeys up the hill. We made a fort in a large hollowed tree in the woods, found scorpions in the side yard, and fished endlessly in the Sunken Garden for tadpoles, pulling out jar after jar of slimy frog eggs.

When it came to playing with Hildi, David refused. Hildi lived on the fourth floor and was shrill and demanding. Her father had long legs and climbed the stairs like a spider. I did not like her one bit, and my mother lectured me on acts of kindness and charity. One afternoon, we sat with a bowl of raisins on the hot asphalt driveway next to the fragrant bay leaf hedges. She lay on her back, her eyes half closed and her mouth open like a small bird. I considered the line of ants walking by. Without thinking, I squeezed an ant into the folds of a raisin and popped it into her mouth. "How does it taste?" I politely inquired. She nodded happily. I tried her on two ants, then three and four. She was happy, and I was, well, pleased.

Between semester breaks and holidays we traveled. We went to the Cappadocia region with its canyons and cones, and to the ancient city of Pergamon in Pergamum. We visited the Temple of Artemis in Ephesus, and the ruins of Sardis, the old capital of the Kingdom of Lydia. We swam in the Black Sea, went to Izmir, and drove through Syria and Lebanon to visit the old city of Jerusalem, which, at that time, was still part of Jordan. My parents' biggest project, however, was to photograph the Crusader castles in the interior of Turkey.

We were an exotic sight. Arriving in a cloud of dust at small villages, we saw farmers drop their tools and children run beside the car, laughing. Women pressed up against us, touching our clothes and skin. My stepfather's height and blue eyes were impressive; he towered over the Turks. Dictionary in hand, my mother gestured and sputtered a few words. *Günaydın,* hello. *Lokanta nerede?* Where is the restaurant? And *teşekkür ederim,* thank you.

One cold spring vacation when I was eight, we drove to the great Crusader castle of Yilhan. It sits solitary on a rock hill, rising out of the rich plain to the west of Adana. Beautifully preserved and remote, the majestic front walls of the castle edge down the side of a cliff. Legends call it "the castle of the snakes" and claim the king's daughter was eaten by snakes.

Yilhan castle was some distance from a small village through deeply rutted muddy roads. The bridge over a small river was only half completed. We slowly forded the waters. The sun was bright, and the fields below were newly plowed and green.

The sun was setting when we climbed to the top of the castle. We edged around the ruins carefully. Many of the centers of the rooms had given out, and the dark holes revealed the floors below. I was cold and terrified. My stepfather laughed and perched me on the edge of a large stone opening to take a picture of me. His camera lens cover dropped, bouncing down, down, down into the darkness.

For the first time since we had been in Turkey, we camped. The return drive would be difficult, and crossing the river uncertain in the dark. I lay in the back seat of the car, lulled by the fire light flickering on the glass. The night was deep and quiet. My parents slept outside.

"Stay down." My mother's breath was hot over the front seat. "Don't let them see you!" She shoved my half-awake body down to the floorboards.

Male voices argued. "*Gasös*," they demanded—a delicious citrus soda drink—and "*Para*," money. Two nomads had seen the campfire and now stood threatening my stepfather with their long shepherd sticks. My mother jumped in the car to start the cranky engine. A man's face appeared in the car window, red and elongated. She wound up the window, trapping his fingers. He yelped as he pulled himself free. My stepfather continued to argue with them. Suddenly they hit him with their sticks. He leaped into the car and we careened off.

The river we had forded that afternoon was a short distance away. My stepfather paused for a moment, and then drove carefully into the water, across the small bar of gravel, and up the other side of the bank. It was steep and muddy, and the tires of the car spun. We slid back into the river to the bar. He tried again, but this time the engine, soaked by water, spluttered and went out. We were silent, trapped in the riverbed on the crest of a small island of gravel. The half-finished bridge stood in front of us. The night was quiet and cold. The horizon had a slight glow to it. Dogs barked in the distance. My stepfather got out the short-handled camping ax from the trunk.

We waited.

The nomads appeared in silhouette on the bridge overlooking us, their clothing whipping about them in the wind. They began pelting us with rocks. The car reverberated with hard, sharp slaps; stones bounced and broke windows. My stepfather got out and threw rocks back. Sitting in the front seat, my mother scribbled notes furiously, describing the attackers. She was certain we would be found in the morning with our throats slit. I burrowed down in my sleeping bag on the floor. I was filled with an odd sense of detachment or maybe adventure; I knew better than to bother my mother with my feelings.

"They've stopped," my stepfather panted as he got back into the car, "for the moment." His hands were red from throwing rocks, his shoulder already stiffening from being hit. The nomads had disappeared. Then the rocks hailed down again, and he returned to keep them back.

Silence again, and the cold gleam of stars. My parents whispered together. We were to make a run for it. Carefully placing my mother's violin ("My Barbie too!" I begged) in the trunk, we scrambled up the slippery edge of the riverbed and followed the road several miles back into the village, stumbling on the frozen ruts of mud.

It was the season of Ramadan. An old man walked the dark streets thumping a large drum, waking villagers so they could eat before the sun was up. We appeared like ghosts, two Americans and a small child. He was speechless. He directed us to the village *muhta*, or justice of the peace. The door opened to a man in pajamas; his wife squatted on the dirt floor by the stove. They put me into what seemed like the softest bed I had ever been in and served my parents tea.

The whole village took care of us over the next few days. They towed the car out of the river, replaced windows, and popped out the dents. They fed and housed us and took us on a visit to the dam being built nearby. In the meantime, the authorities had rounded up the nomads from the area for my parents to identify.

We sat in the police station with the magistrate. The two nomads were brought into the room for a final identification. The taller one had changed his clothing to the typical Turkish dress attire—a white shirt and rich blue pants. The other was dressed in the same yellow ocher coat he'd had on several nights before. His coat was filthy and buttoned wrong, the large buttons recessed deeply into the wool. He was young, his face streaked, and his left eye was covered with the white film of a cataract. My mother nodded her head, yes, these were the two.

I waited on a hard wooden chair next to the wall. The magistrate and my parents talked. The nomads stood erect, their guards slightly behind them. The room was warm, and the dust hung in the air. I closed my eyes as a deep sadness crept over me. They would be sentenced to hard labor, perhaps for years. They were poor, dirty, and had no medical attention or education. The first pangs of empathy and compassion were painful.

We lived joyously in Istanbul for three years. Eva was born in the spring when the nightingales sang, Scott two years later. My mother's mother came to live with us and shared my room. During the school year, I went to an English primary school. Fatima, the maid upstairs, braided my hair so tight my eyes teared. In the summer, my hair was loose and I ran with David in the woods.

We left one beautiful summer afternoon. My stepfather had carefully refashioned the interior of the small car so we could travel and camp for two months. My six-week-old brother's canvas crib was slung between the front and back seats, allowing just enough room for my grandmother and me to sit on either side. Two-year-old Eva sat between my parents in the front seat.

The car was laden with supplies and camping gear. The roof rack was stacked high with suitcases. Students and friends gathered to see us off. We talked and hugged, remembering last-minute things to fetch, and finally, wedged in the car, we drove off trailing goodbyes and tears.

We couldn't bear to leave. Stopping for a final visit to the Grand Bazaar in downtown Istanbul, we ambled through the dark corridors with patches of sunlight, looking at the stalls of rugs, brassware, and jewelry. Vendors leaped at us out of their dark corners to get our attention, gesturing that they had a deal, a really good deal. Small teashops hugged the walls, and men sat at tables with delicate tea glasses grasped in rough hands. I ate halva with pistachios, and Eva rode on my stepfather's shoulders. My mother bought a blue-eyed amulet to protect my baby brother.

It was late when we finally got back on the road. The air was hot and sticky, and red sun slanted into our eyes. Traffic clogged the roads. I had changed places with my mother, who was now wedged in the corner of the back seat, nursing the baby. Eva was sleeping next to me, her neck and back wet with sweat. She sat up, groggy, took a hold of my long hair in her hands, and pulled. I howled.

"Make her stop!" my stepfather snapped.

"I can't!" I twisted and turned. Eva hung on and started to cry as well. Just at that moment, the roof rack, loaded with our baggage, started to slide down the windscreen of the car. He reached up and held on, driving into the now blinding sunset. Turning to my mother, he glared, "I told you we should have taken the boat!"

Later, he cooled Eva off by picking her up and dunking her upside down into a spring of fresh water. My mother repacked the car and got rid of everything that was nonessential.

We traveled and camped the entire summer, sometimes with our good friends, and other times alone. Early in the morning, I played under the olive trees, the thin sun lighting up the silver leaves. My mother cooked breakfast over the camp stove while planning the day's adventures. Eva was cherubic, Scott was plump and laughing. My stepfather emerged from the Mediterranean after an early morning swim like an American Poseidon, his snorkel gear attached to his head, a small sea treasure tucked in his swimming trunks. We were happy.

I still dream of Turkey—the warmth, the color and motion, the blue of the skies and freedom, the family harmony and beauty. Istanbul, my Garden of Eden. We moved through the three years seamlessly, and with the end of summer dropped into the ordinary world of small-town living. The years afterward were long and gray; our home was dark and noisy. To my classmates I was an alien. And my parents, despite the birth of two more children, began to move emotionally and physically away from each other.

We all began to slip into darkness.

Chapter 6

EARTH

Philadelphia (1989)

Go quickly, Tsukiko, into your circled dance.
Janice Mirikitani[1]

January 11

I fly to San Francisco to rehearse with the Kronos Quartet on the new work they commissioned, *Cassandra Sings*. As I travel west, I yearn for this unknown land—flat, large, with sudden great mountains. Lake Tahoe glistens like a sapphire. How little I know this country called home. Suddenly we leave the black hills of Nevada. The plains are brown and neatly squared.

Before I left, Cassie snuggled with me. Asleep, she threw her arm around my neck.

January 14

I stay with composer Jin Hi Kim in her apartment. Her beautiful tiny hands hang in the air for a moment as she looks at me. "If something not working, better fix quick!" she advises me about my music.

The week is black and desolate. In three days, Kronos Quartet have only rehearsed two-thirds of my quartet and have yet to play the whole piece through. Each day they inch through a small section, making almost no progress. I am exhausted.

San Francisco is bone cold, and I take long baths. I call on my child-spirits. They are quick to desert me. They call me names and accuse me of writing a bad piece.

"Calm down," I tell them. Suddenly I see new solutions, new revisions.

January 21

I am back in the air again, this time to Minneapolis. Since coming home from San Francisco, I have revised sections of the quartet and nursed a sick Cassie. At first she hugged me constantly. Then her energy paled and she grew tired and listless, a puddle of illness.

January 22

Finally, Cassandra sang. Kronos Quartet found her.

At the dress rehearsal in the Walker Art Center, they play my piece in an extraordinary manner, with every note of this difficult piece in place—except for the last two, a major third echoed an octave below. I almost laugh out loud. "What's going on with the last two notes?" I ask.

"We felt the ending was too optimistic, so we changed them," the first violinist, David Harrington, explains. I hold my breath and wait. They have several versions to play for me—a minor third, and dissonant second, but nothing seems right.

Finally, the violist says quietly, "Let's play the piece the way it is written."

The performance is brilliant, and I go on stage during the applause. David leans toward me. "I withdraw the argument," he whispers. Next week is the New York City premiere at Alice Tully Hall.

February 8

Black thumbprints are on foreheads. It is Ash Wednesday and the faithful have been to church. The morning in my studio is long. I search for the intensity of writing, that wonderful absorbing feeling of being.

> *I am the earth, I am the root*
> *I am the stem that fed the fruit,*
> *the link that joins you to the night.*[2]

February 10

Lazy days. I am looking at my orchestra piece again, slowly relearning the material. Other than that, I am just resting my composing head.

I am in pain. The tension of the last six months has left me with sharp vertical discomfort down my spine and across my shoulders. My back crackles, and I can't sleep.

March 7

I begin the first of ten sessions of Rolfing, a deep muscle balancing process that realigns the body's structure. I am finally seeking relief after suffering for decades with pain in my back and neck.

Linda Grace is a gray-haired Buddha with warm hands. She lifts my muscles out, separating each from its sheath. I have a feeling of great wonder and sadness to have lived this long without this caring touching. Her hands reach down to each muscle, validate the structure that holds me up.

This body discovery comes with excitement and joy, but also with sadness for my past lack. As a door opens, the light illuminates both the new beauty of the great outdoors and the emptiness of the room I have been living in.

I am reminded of my heart catheterization I had five years ago—the exam room was cool, and I lay under the equipment and overhead monitors. The thin wire was threaded through my artery like a small snake into my heart. As I watched, I was flooded with sudden gratitude. My organs work tirelessly on my behalf, asking nothing of me in return. How am I this fortunate? What a slenderness between life and death, the frailness of the body, and the strength of the spirit! I sank into the deep wonder of the moment.

March 12

I've been procrastinating, hanging back. This week is the time to plunge in and start the orchestra piece. Eventually, I have to leap.

Beginning or restarting a work is difficult. The rush is wonderful when the writing goes well, but remembering the long birth process is disheartening. The music, always absorbing, brings an assortment of joy, sorrow, pleasure, and pain.

For now I enjoy the bliss of waiting, the peaceful sleep before waking. In the morning I turn from the light and snuggle deep in the covers, hoarding the last warmth and sweetness of rest. This is the darkness of rebirth, the Rip Van Winkle sleep and refreshment before the final task: to give of oneself yet again. Here is where doubt reigns, as I face my nascent piece. Sometimes, I imagine what it would be like to stop composing, to let it go, to rest.

The morning winks at me and coaxes me out of bed. I smile, both at the pleasure of waking and the pleasure of sleeping.

March 16

We sit, shoulder to shoulder, listening to her string quartet. Composer Jennifer Higdon is a student at the University of Pennsylvania. She comes over often to share her music or to talk. The afternoon is late, and shadows lengthen through the windows. She is dressed in a dark jacket, her face is open and smiling, framed by short black hair. Her musical style is in the same spirit as mine, a beautiful motif appears and then recedes, ebbing and flowing as it is pushed by rhythms. We wonder out loud what relevance the standard of development has to our music. What does that word mean—*develop*?

I keep hearing the word *allow* instead of *develop*, giving the music room to fill. Is this merely about semantics, or does the argument have a deeper meaning?

In the classical music tradition, development is a process by which a composer uses the musical material of the piece. The melody and accompanying components are reworked, stretched out, condensed, or changed in some fashion throughout the piece. The sonata form uses development as part of the overall structure of the piece, so that whole sections appear again, sometimes slightly modified. The idea is that the listener will anticipate the return of a melody or a section, and even understand the music better because of the repetitions.

Many living composers use development as a chief technique in their music. They push the melodies around and rework them by directly transposing or inverting them. My ear pauses. Why do I feel that they stand at the river's edge, beating their musical material with stones until it is thin, weak, and colorless?

Music, for me, is like bread. I define the ingredients, actively knead the dough. There is an essential part I cannot do—the rising. I provide the right size pan, large enough so the bread can expand to its fullest potential and small enough so it can use the sides of the pan as support. I decide when the bread has risen enough without too much poking around. This is a judgment of my eye, heart, and mind acting together. Rising too much, it will be filled with air and collapse. Rising too little, it will be mean and hard, an impenetrable nugget.

The word *allow* asks for balance and helps me rethink the issue of ownership and parentage. *Allow* provides a medium for growth and questions authority. Too much control forces a finger into sacred ground, leaving a trail of infection. To allow, in the end, is to have.

March 17
Edwina Lee Tyler—composer, drummer, and performer—teaches me. She is small and nut-brown. Vibrant, she is deeply spiritual and sexual. As I listen, I am suddenly in touch with my own private energy, so different from men's. I cannot imitate their postures, the spurting, stumping music coming to an abrupt end. Instead, I write about myself and this dark sexuality. My energy comes from a central place and moves out like the tide. It grows and expands; it becomes an entity. My sexuality is wide and continuous. It passes through, envelops, and sustains in long waves of water.

"My drum is a woman," Edwina says.

March 27
I sit in the therapist's office with my sister Eva. I look out a window onto the barn outside. The siding is weathered gray-brown,

green with moss and lichen. The barn is stark and cold, like my childhood. The couch is enveloping. I take off my shoes and curl my feet under me. I both bare my feet and hide them. We are trying to make some sense of this childhood we share, our current distance and anger with each other.

The afternoon is long and the therapist pauses. Finally she lifts her head. "What would you lose if you stop fighting?" she asks. Sound recedes and I am alone. I only see the image of my stepfather.

I do not understand. I would lose my stepfather, lose his love—something I never had? Have I always blamed Eva for being his favorite? Been jealous of his attentiveness to her, the light that was so apparent in his face when she came into view?

I soften. My anger at her has been a placeholder for his neglect—the last vestige and final hope of getting his attention.

March 28

"Don't you remember?" asks my youngest brother, Loren, his voice in my ear on the phone.

Late one summer, my stepfather was leaving for his yearly training as an Army reservist. His brother, Uncle Harrison, was to drive him to the airport, and we had gathered around for a final goodbye. Going from child to child my stepfather kissed everyone. But not me.

Turning bright red, my uncle immediately objected, and soon the brothers were in a heated argument that erupted into blows.

I am blank. I have no recollection of this.

LET YOUR HEART BE BROKEN

April 1

Last night the cat scampered over the bed, waking me. Eva's beautiful slender fingers hover in front of me. I am filled with desire both to possess and be possessed by these hands. How much I keep from you! How could you know how deeply affected I have been by the adoption and my sense of being an outsider? I hide so much from you; I kept so much from myself.

"People don't change. They stand more revealed,"[3] writes poet Charles Olson. I stand uncovered and am disquieted. I am ashamed of my pink, vulnerable, pitiful flesh. My eyes are downcast. I shift my weight from foot to foot. I am red and shiny, a glistening crab body. Who loves such a girl? Certainly not Mother, definitely not Father. Perhaps Eva, enemy of my flesh. If we are one, I will belong. I will have crossed over.

April 3

My music is an experience, not an event. Most music is circular and contained. Mine, on the other hand, is languid and rests on its elbows like a horizon. I create a linear shape where the music evolves, transforms, and becomes. The listener moves with the music through a passage of time into another place. In the end, the music breaks open like an egg, its content finally revealed. The gift is the inner and outer, the private and public. The soul unveiled.

April 12

I go to my weekly Rolfing session. My back is full of heat and pain. We talk about the years of playing piano and composing. Idly, Linda Grace asks if I had a strict piano teacher as a child, or if someone made me tense while I played. She works in silence, and

68

my mind wanders back to Istanbul. Suddenly I sit up gasping; a memory, carefully lodged in my back, has come flooding out.

I am eight, possibly nine. I am at my piano lesson, playing a Burgmüller étude. My teacher sits at the other piano and listens. Her husband comes silently out of the back room. I know him; he is my mother's violin teacher. He is always home when I come to lessons and she is not there yet.

He leans over my shoulder and playfully points out a mistake I made. As he talks, he slowly rubs his penis into my back. This is not the first time.

My back is a thick and tough turtle shell, hardened around the site of his sexual abuse. The Rolfing reaches through my shield and touches the hidden vulnerability. I weep all day.

April 13

I have only snapshots of memory. One of my schoolteachers walks me to my piano lesson, delivering me at the door of my piano teacher's apartment. She is always late; I am always early. I ascend the long staircase to the apartment where her husband waits for me, ready to reach under my dress. He has me touch his penis, red and soft to my hand. Often my underpants are inexplicably wet.

I have no idea how long this goes on. He speaks no English and gestures to me, making me promise not to tell anyone. I am frightened and confused. Only when we return to America did I tell my mother. She nodded sympathetically. "Don't tell anyone," she advised.

I do not understand. I knew this. I screamed at him in therapy, yanked his tie, pulling him down to my child face. "You will never do this to me again," I spat.

And yet, here, years later, hidden in my back, lodged this memory—a final insult. I am physically ill.

April 16

The child is in pain. I lay my hands on either side of her spine. Her back is thin, vulnerable; the injury is deep.

There are little holes on either side of my spine, just below the shoulder blades. You can only touch them by reaching up from under. They are hidden, a secret path through my back: *the fifth chakra is in the neck and represents openness to the world.*

April 19

The orchestra piece moves smoothly. Who would have thought two weeks ago I was in such a state of paralysis?

Orchestration is wonderful and challenging. It is like making finely balanced cake, where too much or too little frosting ruins the delicate taste. I trace each section back to its most elemental, then start to layer the lines carefully. If I lose the thread, I double back and start again to find it.

May 19

Kronos Quartet performed the last performance of my piece. They played better than ever, and the slow section bloomed and blossomed. In the last two days, two more commissions have come in. The new challenges both excite and worry me.

July 22

I pack for our month at the shore, trying to remember all the things that Cassie and I will need. Wood will stay and work. He has found a new job at a local hospital and is away for long periods of time.

The Mantoloking house calls to me; I look forward to the long period of quiet and peace but have a measure of worry. I must trust myself more.

The orchestra piece is almost complete. The calm intensity that I have had since mid-May continues. When I work intently over a long period of time, I lose track of things like bills, phone calls, or news. I feel addled, dull, as if I didn't have anything to say. I am often times confused and have to stop and think, as if I had a brain impediment. As I complete the piece, I emerge out of the water. First my eyes appear, then my nose, till slowly I walk up onto the beach. The new piece for Sylmar Ensemble has begun to gnaw at me—I know I will land it soon.

August 9

The days down at the shore pass gloriously. I am overjoyed at the reading and the thinking. Cassie clamors for my attention because I am constantly distracted—I escape into books or my writing, always snatching a few moments of unguarded time. I am a better parent when I've had eight hours to myself and can let my work go completely when we are reunited. Cassie is delicious when I've had a whole day to work. Continuous, unrelieved deliciousness, however, is tiring.

I fight sleep and stay up late at night so I can get in a few more hours. As I turn off the light, I smell the phantom aroma of morning coffee and anticipate the pleasure of the morning, the excitement of a new day full of offerings.

August 10
All night I dream of Istanbul.

How is it that Istanbul rises like a gleaming tower in my memory, untarnished? Certainly, it was a time of harmony between my mother and my stepfather, their faces animated over shared interests. And I was unfettered and ran unchecked on the plateau or in the deep woods.

Moreover, I had by then learned the fine art of sublimation. I happily detached from being attacked by nomads or molested by my piano teacher's husband. I blacked them out with darkness and clung to the light.

August 14
How do I negotiate the space between two differences without my intuition or my intellect? I am so often sandwiched in between the two that I do not notice there is a third way around: a leap, over an abyss, over the width to a tangible path.

August 21
I am bad tempered and thwarted today. I hired a babysitter to care for Cassie in the mornings, but he has disappeared. I lurch around for time to write.

Cassie clings to me. She complains, "I'm so bad, Momma, I'll never do anything right." I am impatient and foolishly add fuel to her flame.

August 24
The sun is bright and warm, the sky luminous and blue, the wind cool and refreshing. I am reading Joseph Campbell's *The Inner*

Reaches of Outer Space, Metaphor as Myth and as Religion. Cassie plays quietly, coming over for a hug.

We enjoy our last few days here. The hours pass quickly while she is with the babysitter, and I am happy at her return. Next week we will be home. The knowledge that I will have time to myself makes these last few days more enjoyable.

I have an idea for a new piece. Several months ago, I dreamed a quartet was playing a piece of mine with a string orchestra. The piece was haunting. As I woke, the lines of T. S. Eliot's poem were in my ear, "I have heard the mermaids singing, each to each."[4] Somehow this will be part of the new piece.

I asked Cassie how a mermaid might sound, and we sang softly in echoes. The next day she asked, "Have you written the piece yet?"

September 1

I love and hate beginnings. I have cleaned off my desk (written thousands of letters) and vacuumed my studio (thrown out thousands of magazines). Now the work sits there. It is time to start the next piece—*Blue Dawn [The Promised Fruit]*. The Navajo associate blue with fructifying power of the earth, with water, with sky. I stall.

Marc Chagall wrote, "In my paintings I have hidden my love." Why does he *hide* his love? In my work, I want my love to pour out.

The phone rings, Minneapolis Composers Forum will commission me to write a piece for youth orchestra.

September 7
Work begins on *Blue Dawn*. My ear is off; old melodies keep running through my head. Nothing is fresh. I keep listening. I am restless. "Listen!" I shout to myself. Instead, I watch TV, take a long walk, do anything to keep the day moving. I can't read. I sit in the park, and finally, it comes. I still need to create the material, but the organization, the shape, and the sound is there.

September 8
Annie Dillard, in *A Writing Life,* puts her finger on it.

> One of the few things I know about writing is this: spend it all, shoot it, play it, lose it, all, right away every time. Do not hoard what seems good for a later place in the book, or for another book; give it, give it all, give it now ... Something more will arise later, something better. These things fill in from behind, from beneath, like well water. Similarly, the impulse to keep to yourself what you have learned is not only shameful, it is destructive. Anything you do not give freely and abundantly, becomes lost to you. You open your safe and find ashes. [5]

You open your safe and find ashes.

September 10
I heard a piece by composer Jim Tenney recently at a concert. Something interests me. His piece is a voyage of technical manipulations involving tape delay and difference tones—those

haunting resonances that appear when certain pitches rub against each other.

At first I am rapt. But I cannot hold on. My mind disengages and falls into a dark quiet. After eight to ten minutes, the piece suddenly opens up, and I catch onto the piece again. How did I get here—where have I been? As if a white shirt, shown in meticulous technical detail, suddenly blossoms with blood, both a terrifying signal of death and an affirmation of life.

The shape of his music reminds me of my own shape. While the content of our work is different, the linear shape and flow, moving from one point to (and through) another, is similar. He uses a one-theme-one-idea approach, where the starkness and persistence engages the listener. I am episodic, darting though material with single-minded purpose. His music is a straight line, mine moves in and over. He takes a fragment and expands it. I sew my fragments together, so one becomes another becomes one. His overall shape is like the stem of a flower, long and thin with a sudden bloom at the end. My shape is conical; the whole piece expands from a beginning point and opens up to an ecstasy. His epiphany is sharply beautiful in relief to his material. Mine is joyous and circular.

October 12
Suddenly cold and beautiful. I work in the garden and later go to a concert. Cassie plays with friends. I plunge ahead with *Blue Dawn*. I finish the last three minutes first. It shimmers like an opening. The work pulses softly, draping itself around the inner core.

October 16

Monday is always a reprieve. All weekend I itch to write my piece. When I am writing well, I leave my studio on Friday afternoon determined not to write for the weekend. I know I need the time off. But I tread water. I wander into my studio and look at the music on my desk, edgy and disconsolate. The days pass as if marking time, without purpose.

October 17

Another cold and rainy day. The light is pale and thin in my studio. I start the first section of the piece. I pace in the rain, heavily. I nap for an hour, waking half hallucinating, half dreaming. The piece turns slowly in my ear. The opening is like the opening of a flower.

November 15

The New Music America Festival at the Brooklyn Academy of Music is amazing in the breadth of music it presents, with many crossover bands, jazz, and experimental new music composers. The iconic and reclusive Conlon Nancarrow comes for a concert of his music. He writes exclusively for the player piano, both to get rid of human discrepancy and to manage his difficult rhythms and dispassionate music. His single-minded insistence to write his own vision is powerful.

Performance artist Karen Finley mesmerizes, her voice shifting and calling out. She personifies the abuses of women, wailing out their anguish. Jerry Hunt, tall and thin, performs for a large audience of children. He moves rapidly around the stage, shaking his rattles and beating the suitcases with wands while making strange movements. Always a comedian, he quips, "A third of the children were in over their heads, a third of them were insulted, and a third of them were interested to the point of boredom."

As the President of the New Music Alliance, I am in many meetings, developing the next year's festival in Montreal over the ten days. The plans are extraordinary.

November 20
I come home weak and symptomatic. I have clearly done more than my heart can accommodate. I catch up on correspondence, try to do a little writing, and stay in bed resting.

December 2
Secretly, I am pessimistic. I wake, take a shower, cough, and am exhausted. I want to slide back into bed and sleep it out. Often emotional, I cry while reading Cassie a story.

My time living with congestive heart failure is at a crisis. It has been almost eight years, and my heart is tired and enlarged. Wood and I discuss the possibility of a valve repair instead of a replacement. There are only two doctors in the US who do the newly developed procedure.

Cassie plays nearby and chimes in. "I have that too, just like Mommy!" She laughs happily.

I must get out of my emotional stasis. By Monday I want to be working on music again, so I can feel the future, so that I don't sink slowly into inactivity.

December 6
The roller-coaster ride continues, up and down with my health and long-term surgery plans. Last week I hadn't significantly

improved. After a long, bitter cry, I felt more like myself. The tide is shifting.

December 20

The day is cold and snow blown. The sun shines clear on the stark, naked trees. The house is bright with reflection. We rest inside, warm from the white, frosty day.

Last night I dreamed of the earth. Slowly I descend through a crack and sit on a rock that glows with an inner gold. A black underground lake glistens; I move toward a red light. I swim, searching for something. Light filters through the dusty water; the bottom is covered with gray-green silt, undisturbed for centuries. Large, prehistoric fish appear and disappear, dark plants wave, rocks loom. Suddenly the water is filled with phosphorescent light, and blue-green iridescent shapes blossom. They hang in the water for a moment, then close.

My music is like these open underwater creatures revealing their bright moist interior like a dark round womb; an undulating, ruby red, glistening secret.

Life is all I know, but it seems so small compared to the fathomless unknowns. My work in the last four years has an inner understanding that allows for outer clarity and distinction. My professional achievements are less than my growing connection to all of life—the earth, the fire (glow), the water (lake), and air. The purpose of my music, this outer manifestation of myself, is the inner connectedness. Music, like life, is no more than itself. There is no implicit reason to it except that it is. And that is its magic. Like swimming in a dark underground grotto, life miraculously pulses open.

The intent is to be, to speak, to reveal myself. I need not to change the world, but merely resonate with others. That is enough. My dedication is to stay open so that the music—so that I—can be found. Like the dark lake with silt-covered rocks, durable, ageless, and constant. In that, the ego has no claim or stake.

My illness and the presence of possible death put this all into sharp focus. At times I would gladly give in to rest. Yet, as I descend into the earth, the ledges glow like the streams of love from my neighbors and friends. This intensity lifts my heart and extends me outward. I sink into the earth of my own soul and am illuminated by others. The earth is horizontal, mute, ageless, and cool; love is vertical, noisy, animate, and warm.

Immobility is fear itself: fear to live in death, fear to be grounded, fear of the stretch to the sky, fear to live with intent but without ego, fear to accept the gift of warmth, and fear of love. Fear to be as I am, to do as I must.

The earth offers me strength and timelessness. Human love offers me flexibility and energy to touch the sky. I bring to these my offerings of trembling courage.

Chapter 7

IF TRUTH BE TOLD

My mother is beautiful, with raven hair cropped in a fifties short style, black eyes, dramatic eyebrows, and red, red lipstick. I sit on her bed, my skinny legs bouncing back and forth on the side like white flags, watching her dress for a party. I am four, perhaps five.

She pauses to say something to me, sprays a perfume cloud to walk through. Her dark hair falls against creamy skin. A beautiful tulle strapless dress that she had meticulously sewed frames her small waist. Her shoulders are bare and beautiful. I breathe her in.

How had I been so fortunate to have been found by this woman?

❧

For years I had no memories of anything before I was three and a half. The world is dark, and then suddenly it is light. I lived in the south of Sweden in a foster home. Solvig, I was told, was my foster mother, and Torsten, my foster father. My mother, in Sweden for a year-long lectureship, adopted me in the summer of

1956. She returned with me to her first job as a college professor in Athens, Ohio.

We moved into a large house on top of a steep hill, with a backyard that dropped off sickeningly into a tiny stream. I was the pixie child with dark laughing eyes, and she was a smart young woman with a future. I only spoke Swedish, and we conversed quickly with each other in a melodious fall and dip. When I learned a word in English, I never used the equivalent Swedish again. I firmly put away the language of my memories and moved forward.

Over the next seven years my mother and stepfather had four children. Eva and Scott arrived during the years in Istanbul. Lâle was born shortly after returning to the states, followed by a long pause. Loren, named after my stepfather, was born in cold January of 1964.

My adoption was never spoken about. All through my younger years I was merely the oldest of five. Secretly, I was acutely aware of the difference. I assumed my stepfather's last name but knew my legal name on my passport was my mother's maiden name, Aney. And while we tumbled through our childhood good naturedly, occasionally one of my siblings taunted, "You're just adopted."

I was ten when I learned the potency of the word. I stood in our narrow, shadowy kitchen washing dishes with my back to my mother. Plunging my hands into the soapy water, I asked, "Does adoption mean that the parents have died or didn't want their child?" Trying to put it together. I glanced over my shoulder. Her face was stricken and white.

"I thought you knew what adopted meant?" she said hoarsely.

I never brought up the subject again.

In my mind, I romanticized it. Being born in Sweden, I imagined that my parents were tall, beautiful, and blond. It was hard for me to explain my dark hair. With visions of little orphan Annie, I cheerfully considered I had been rescued from an orphanage, saved from a life of penury and hardship.

The only other person I knew who was adopted was Gladys, the daughter of my stepfather's parents. A few years older than I, Gladys was found dirty and malnourished in a shack with her alcoholic parents. Although my grandparents were old, they took her in.

Gladys was full of fantasy and always had a story going on while she did the chores around the house. She was a captured princess who was forced to work as a servant, or a beautiful maid hired by a family whose handsome son was in love with her. When we played in the timbered barn, she was a lifeguard who rescued me as I swam in the hay. Late at night she showed me her first long pubic hair and the soft fuzz of her armpits.

Gladys often hung onto my stepfather's large frame and made a show of it in front of me. "You are adopted." She smiled at me, leaning on him as he squatted on the ground. "But I'm not." He did not contradict her, and I knew I could not lean on him with such ease.

Being adopted was precarious. There were no second chances. I worked hard and became indispensable. Having no body memory of my own, I lived on borrowed family history. And constantly there was a secret dread that one day a knock would echo through the house, and I would have to leave again.

I returned to Sweden in the summer of my twenty-first year. The Chance family asked me to accompany their daughter, Lillie, as she started a year abroad. At thirteen she was gangly and caustic.

In a quiet section of Stockholm on Östermalmsgatan, we lived with family friends of Lillie's parents. The Baltschefskys were away for most of the summer and so, we found out quickly, was almost everyone in Stockholm during the vacation months. We spent two lonely months learning Swedish and exploring an empty city.

At the end of my stay, I was determined to find out about my adoption. I talked to Meg Baltschefsky about it one afternoon when they were in town. Tall and willowy, she had a habit of closing her eyes when she said something important. "Yes," she encouraged, her eyes blinking. "You should find out about yourself."

On the phone, the Swedish adoption agency patiently explained that they never allowed a national to be adopted by a foreigner, even in the 1950s. They were sure they didn't have any information but would look. Confused, I turned to the American Embassy. Another dead end. They had no records on hand, and older files were in storage. Did I want to make a request? It would take months. Discouraged, I waited.

Just before flying back home, I called the Swedish agency again. The woman on the phone was relieved and apologetic. She had information. "Please, come down immediately." *They had died, they were still alive. They wanted and loved me. They couldn't remember me. They never forgot about me.* My mind tumbling, I brushed past Meg. "I'm going to find out about my birth parents," I called on my way out.

The adoption agency office was dark and small. Fröken Karlsson sat at her desk looking through my file. She asked questions about my life as she sorted through papers. Where had I lived after my three years with the Elmståhls family, and did I have any siblings?

Finally she pulled a single page out; a letter my mother had written when she adopted me. I could see the traces of the handwriting through the paper as Fröken Karlsson read it out loud to me.

I had been adopted by my birth mother.

There was a long silence. Adopted by my birth mother. My world tilted, receded. My adopted mother was my birth mother? I sat there.

"Are you all right?" she asked kindly.

"Of course," I murmured.

I made my way back to the apartment. "My parents died," I lied. "There was not much information. An accident…" My voice trailed off. Meg looked long at me, her eyes deep brown and open.

The next day I packed. I returned to America. I started my junior year of college. Frozen.

For twenty-one years I lived as an adopted child, with a body ache for my origins, a deep sense of separateness. Now, a sleight of hand, a substitution of words, had changed my landscape forever.

What is truth or reality? A hard fact? A principle? *In actual fact, as it happens, in point of fact, in reality, really, actually, if truth be told?[1]* Facts are word-dependent. Pluto was a planet until we found out recently that it was not. Pluto was never a planet.

My mother was the brave adoptive parent of a lively three-year-old Swedish girl. Actually, she was a heartsick, abandoned woman of an ill-fated love affair. I had been saved and found by generosity and love. In truth, I was unnamed and hidden. I was an illegitimate child.

What had my mother been thinking? Did she wish to protect herself and me? Life in the '50s was not kind to women. She could have possibly forfeited her job, reputation, and ability to care for me. Or perhaps she thought this secret was private, and that privacy did not include me.

The difference, however, between private and secret is worlds apart. We are all entitled to privacy; but a secret, a small untruth, even for the best of reasons, begins to have a life of its own. It becomes a monster, a personal Frankenstein without a conscience. He runs amok, clacking and clanging in everyone's closet. Slowly seeping upward like bad groundwater, he poisons the well. Then returning again and again, he binds you in the straitjacket of your own devising. You are imprisoned.

A world hangs in the difference of words. We are the stories we tell about ourselves and the stories told to us. That summer in Sweden marked a dividing line between what I thought I knew and what there was to know. A world of grief opened up for me, and I struggled to place the pieces together and to remember. And I had to endure my rage and learn to forgive.

Chapter 8

HEART

Philadelphia (1989-1990)

If you say no to a single factor in your life, you have unraveled the whole thing. The demon that you swallow gives you its power, and the greater life's pain, the greater life's reply.

Joseph Campbell[1]

December 28

I have been in a malaise, my thoughts and feelings chilled and slow. How do I live with the threat of death, knowing that there is, in the end, nothing? *Amor fati*—love my fate.

December 30

Last night—no, it was early morning—the soft Florida rain fell on the palm leaves outside our tent on our Christmas vacation. Cassie and I walk down the beach away from the campsite while Wood drowses.

The morning skies are cloudy, with an occasional opening of clear blue. A beautiful birthday morning, cool, refreshing. An obscured vista with promise breaking through.

My wish is to release fear and reawaken to the wonders of the moment. My inner children's voices grow louder. They call out to me, reminding me.

At twilight, the blue moon is in its first crescent.

January 5

All of this is hard to write about. I find myself re-experiencing the details of the past two months without conclusion: a quick physical decline, emotional and intellectual chaos, immobilization, my fear of the future. A spiritual crisis, filled with despair and paralysis.

In the cold of December, in the cold fear of my body, I grappled to understand. How could I, who went through this before, who weathered eight years of congestive heart failure, who adjusted so well, who made so many concessions to her health, be back at the start? Worse, I now doubt the meaning and future of my life. While I dream of the earth and accept the joys my daughter affords, while my work becomes more than I ever imagined, I feel utterly abandoned. The thought that this illness might result in me forever leaving my daughter chills me. "The process of dying is a process of recommitment to life," [2] Kübler-Ross says.

My eyes lift. I experience a moment of breathlessness. In this thirty-seventh year, I will find ways to reconnect and recommit myself to life, to open my heart and live. Edging up to this task, what I must learn waits for me.

January 10

Is it possible I never accepted my illness, never let it into my house?

My heart ailment wanders like the lost child of my dreams, sad and ugly. I control, maintain, and concede to it, but never accept it. Always on the outside of me, I am not the heart patient but the one with a heart problem. The hassle is between "who I am" and "I am a victim." In my mind, my heart is ill. I am not. Yet, to ostracize my illness keeps it all the more dangerous.

I treat my illness the way I was treated as a child. I fear it, for it contains the truth. I cast it out, for its presence is painful to me. Denying its existence the way my mother denied mine, I perpetrate a system that nearly destroyed me years ago. It stands to destroy me again.

January 11

The healing meditations suggested by Stephen Levine are difficult. I bumble along. Closing my eyes and focusing my attention downward, I send love to my heart. But it is not where it should be, not left of center. My heart is somehow outside my body, clinging to my side.

Who is ill? Who is the heart? Who is the illness? If Levine is correct, the path and the answers are within me.

Lately I have been sensing the *other*, or the spiritual. A teasing sarcasm leaps up, but my body trusts and accepts. My mind rushes to judge; my arms soften. I am small before this body sense.

I am intrigued (and doubtful) about sending love to others. A recent experience with a local music publisher sent me into a rage. After wrangling over the ownership of my orchestra piece, she refused to print the score and parts, almost costing me the performance of the premiere. For weeks I was caught in a cycle of obsessive thinking and reliving the experience. My mental activity assuaged my humiliation, but only temporarily.

The other day, I drove past her office and felt the tip of the rage again. Instead I sent love. I laughed. What a perfect, unexpected revenge! Then my body was filled with a relaxing. Sending love instead of feeling rage eased me.

Oh, Tina! Who are you—Jesus Christ? Hmm. I am doubtful. But consider this: Last year I imagined the love from my friends and family lifting my body and calming my heart. It was palpable.

Here is what I know: Fundamental knowledge and understanding is always present and available. There is a certain amount of cosmic stuff, for the lack of a better word, that anyone can gain access to. Author Stephen Levine does not give me the path and I don't leap onto his bandwagon. I was ready and caught his book as it fell off the shelf.

At the foot of a dark path of an unexplained discovery, I pause. I find a lamp in my hand.

January 16

Small things please me these days: moments of gold sunlight in the morning, the curve of a branch, dried roses still on the bush, brown broken leaves.

The kindness meditation makes me weep. A terrible sadness of mysterious origins weighs me down. When I say, "May I be free of suffering," I feel as if I have never admitted to it. I have managed the many abuses of my body, spirit, and emotions by keeping them carefully separated. To feel them collectively threatens to blot me out in a second. Yet, when I call to my suffering, I sense more than myself. I am part of a large universal anguish, like enormous black clouds.

January 18

Composing *I Hear the Mermaids Singing* reminds me that my mermaids are not those who lure sailors to erotic death on the rocks. Instead, they are the mermaids of my own deep sexual nature. At ease with watery depth, the unknown and fathomless, they are wild and untamed. Their natural sexual energy is tenderness.

What is sex? The desire to couple with another, to be united. What are mermaids? Our whole impulse, curiosity, and fullness to life. A symbol of feminine wisdom and connectedness, they have access to the "dark and magic underwater world from which our life comes."*3*

January 20

I dream rhythms this morning, undulating and pressing forward. A snake slips across the desert, each scale a separate motion like diamonds fitting together. Sensing a stone ahead, he adjusts his direction immediately. The movement is like lightning, a triumph of small separate motions, synchronized for speed and accuracy.

February 1

The other day, I took Cassie to the zoo. Arriving at the lion cage just after feeding time, we watched two lions in separate cages. Standing squarely on four legs, the male began to bellow. The vibrations rumbled out of him from deep inside; his head circled with the sound. Soon the female joined with vocal thrusts. Her groans came straight from her hips as if she were vomiting. For a long time they roared back and forth. Suddenly they stopped.

February 3

My echocardiogram was at Hahnemann Hospital. The sound waves bouncing through my chest revealed that the blood flowing from my lungs to my heart was poor. The news is not positive, and I am scheduled to have a catheterization at the end of the month. Surgery, while indicated, is not on an emergency basis. I am grateful for the time to prepare.

The sound of my heart fills me with dread. Long gone are the patient little lub-dubs, replaced by a laborious whooshing and sloshing. At night my heart sounds like an enormous boiler cranking away in the dark cellar. I turn over quickly so I can't hear the echoes through the mattress. It is a constant reminder that my faithful servant labors with terrible injury.

February 7

My piece *I Hear the Mermaids Singing* is coming along well. The work is rapid, and I try not to do too much in a day.

The issue of complexity has come up. I was recently criticized for writing "too thin" and am struggling to understand this comment better. *Complex*, at best, is elaborate, intricate, or knotty. At worst, it is an intellectual overlaying that serves only itself. It becomes baffling and chaotic—a great hiding place for us artists.

I write directly; my music is clear, not simplistic. I work to create unity between the parts where, in the growth of the piece, several individual voices become one. The piano is the rhythmic and harmonic core. The viola and cello play haunting slivers of songs. The floating, disembodied voices are surrounded by persistent rhythm until finally they fuse and unite.

February 8

The Harrisburg Symphony did a fine performance of *In the Darkness I Find a Face (It is Mine)*. The conductor was generous with his time and comments, the players enthusiastic and warm.

I learned much, and that in itself is thrilling. The work needs editing and some re-orchestration; I have detailed plans. I am full of good energy.

February 26

The weather grows icy cold after a couple weeks of warmth. I am relieved. I need dormancy.

At night I wake constantly, both from the pain in my back and from my dreams. I am exhausted even while sleeping, as if I am in the middle of an intense work-related experience. I wake to a single lucid thought. *I must change how I relate to music, or, my music must change.* Almost immediately I fall back to sleep, only to do it again.

Since the beginning of the month, I have been sliding into my new piece. The process of writing *I Hear the Mermaids Singing* is unusual for me. The work eases out without much planning. I like it. It is strange to be writing without controlling everything.

I float and observe myself. I am not terribly excited, nor am I impatient. I am receiving a message I do not understand.

March 6

These days are dark and quiet, filled with composing. I have finished *I Hear the Mermaids Singing,* and I wait before copying the pencil score on the computer.

I feel more deeply and personally connected to music than ever before. I live in a world of sound; my ears are filled. When I look up from my work, the house is surprisingly calm, the street empty; the magnolia tree waits to blossom. Looking down again, my ears are flooded.

Sound has never kept me so entranced, so excited. My days are effortless. I am full. Before I touched the surface; now I bathe in the waters. I put my head down in the cool depth and breathe.

Cats are wandering in and out of my dreams. I work on relaxing for the catheterization procedure next week. The results will tell me when I need the open-heart surgery.

March 14

I copy music in the morning, drink coffee, talk to my friend, and transplant the small seedlings in the garden. I clear off my desk.

March 21

The catheterization was, perhaps, the single most terrifying experience of my life. At first everything was in control, although painful. The initial cut down to the femoral artery tugged at my groin muscles, and slowly the catheters were threaded up into my heart. One of them was faulty and was removed. The second catheter was kinked or twisted; I felt a bulge as it went up into the artery curving into my heart.

Suddenly I was a heart beating over two hundred beats a minute. Quietly but frantically they called for the chief doctor to come in—my dear Dr. Gary Mintz. He rushed in, his white coat flapping. He calmly removed the catheter and threaded the third catheter in as if it were made of fine silk. The beating broke to a normal rhythm.

We struggled on through the procedure, my heart slipping into tachycardia again and again, punctuated by long, terrible pauses. I felt the doctors tense up, ready to pounce.

The next couple of days are fragile. My trust is shaken. I imagine my heart will fail. I call Dr. Mintz. My voice quivers on the phone, "Are you sure I won't have a heart attack?"

"I am sure," he says. Then calm. Then letting go of the frantic beating of my heart.

In the quiet moments of panic, I have an image of being dragged, nails screeching, out of my body. I struggle out through a long black tunnel to the sun.

The catheterization has knocked loose dreams, thousands of them, only half remembered or recognized.

April 21
I worry that my marriage is in trouble. My husband has always provided a sheltering place for me to grow, a cold frame protecting me from the cold of my own winter. But now it is spring, early spring.

May 23
Last night was full of dreams and images, a blessing and a relief. For some time my nights have been blank emptiness, or vague fleeting snapshots. I feel dried, as if I had no inner substance. But last night, hundreds of pictures danced in my dreams. I grabbed them as a starving person grabs food, an oasis of dreams.

My restlessness stems from not knowing what is going on in my marriage. I am caught between an awakened desire to have a better relationship and utter lack of imagination of how that might be. I stumble and feel discontent.

My new piece, *Woman Dreaming*, reflects my current state. I have trouble hearing the piece because it is precisely about having and not, about power and sharing, about anger and energy. I dream myself into existence, like the earth slowly gathering energy. Turning black dirt into life, it emerges without scales, iridescent.

I am unsure and must double back. Dreaming myself in fits and starts. I do not understand the line between anger and energy. I pause to comfort myself—I cannot make a straight line to the shining self I wish to be.

May 25

I have cut my hair; the long black tresses are gone. I feel lightened. My clothes are drab and worn. I have spent the last year in a kind of dormant hiding and now need new clothes. It is time to emerge.

June 6

I resist beginning the new piece. And life surrounds me at every step, wanting me to sink back into inertia. I must start spinning.

The week has been relatively calm, and the tensions have decreased. Yet we are fragile. Despite the growing gestures of affection and my husband's cheerfulness, the boat is leaky, rocky.

August 23

Woman Dreaming is finished, copied, and sent out to the Pittsburgh New Music Ensemble. I am sick again, with days of coughing and weakness. Sometimes I am in a panic, other times I am pettish and sorry for myself. I have spent the past two weeks in or near bed, sleeping, reading, or resting, allowing myself to be cared for. It is both difficult and wonderful; I hate and love it. The patience illness takes is endless. A daily lesson.

Often, I am in a fury. I am mad for days at the relentless

attack on my health. At the same time, I know it is my parcel of life, my slice of the celestial heaven. In rare moments, I am grateful to my illness; it throws love and empathy of life into sharp relief.

August 24

Music is a strange business, and I continually try to understand my relationship to it. Paradoxes abound.

Music is all me, but as it sweeps through my life, it becomes other. While not a message from a higher source, it comes out of a deep knowledge. I alone am the source of my music, but it is not me. It comes out of my body but is not my body. The notes flow out of me, but I am not the notes, nor do I own them. In some strange way, I am the servant.

My job is simply to compose. I struggle not to take credit or be personally exalted. A human failing, the desire to be counted. When I am well balanced, I am not a slave but an honored worker. I lie down and offer myself through the music.

October 11

The days go by. I do not compose much. My open-heart surgery will be in six weeks. I find myself in the present, enjoying little moments. When I think of the future, I get tight and breathless. So I relax and take each day as it comes.

Few times have been as quietly peaceful and full. Good moments are gleaming and open; bad moments are dull but passing. I have more pleasure in the single moment than I can remember, as if I have finally learned to linger and enjoy. There is sadness, too, but it comes out of sweetness. Time is like the softest velvet skin of a newborn that will eventually turn hard and protective.

I amble and wait. I work on revisions, I hold my beloved child tight to me. At night, I reach out and stroke my husband's neck. This is a good time. I enjoy it with patience and optimism.

October 25

The moments of panic pass quickly. I am overcome with emotions frequently, but they too are felt and released.

After almost two months of not composing I begin to revise *Cassandra Sings*. The string quartet is wonderful, but the troubling middle section needs tending to. I fall into the sounds again with pleasure. How nice to be "inside" the hours of sound—a world rotating on its own—tangible shapes and vistas. A whole house of sounds. The work makes waiting for the operation bearable. It wakes in me the yearning to have this part of my life over so I can start the next new piece.

"Now I will tell you plainly and from no cryptic speech," says Cassandra in *Agamemnon*, "bear me then witness, running at my heels upon the scent of these old brutal things done long ago. There is a choir that sings as one..."[4]

The moment of singing, of the total self, the richness and the poverty, the joys and the sorrows, the weeping and the laughter, the music and the silence. Singing life as a woman.

November 7

This is the three-week mark to the day of my surgery. I am panicked, my stomach is tight all day. I institute a futuristic mode of accounting—three weeks from today I will be sitting in the hospital bed recovering from the valve repair. Tomorrow, in three weeks' time, a day after the operation, I will be on my feet and walking. It helps me to calm down and focus on the positive.

I finish my revisions of the string quartet and put the orchestration of Schubert's *Fugue* for piano four-hands on the computer. I am almost ready to give my husband my power of attorney and rewrite my will.

The past few months have brought a renewed sense of love and connection to others. As I view the possibility of death, I am aware of an immense feeling of love. I do not anticipate loss but love. When I think of my family, my siblings and relatives, my friends and neighbors, I feel their presence and our connection. The immediacy is light and joyful. I smile at the flow. We breathe in and out together.

I am deeply tired, both physically and psychologically. Stress and illness dull the mind and strip away unnecessary thoughts and feelings. I understand less these days; I feel more.

Last night the three of us ate chicken with walnuts and pomegranates for dinner. We quietly talked and sat silent. How simple and lovely.

November 25

Soon. The operation will be in three days. I take Cassie to the shopping mall to look at the Christmas decorations. A large jazz band plays Christmas songs, and we wiggle through the crowd to sit on the floor. As we listen, Cassie wraps her arm around my neck. The music surges; she turns and kisses me passionately. How could I have lived so much?

I am brought to terror about the upcoming surgery. But wait. Last week I lay on the bed meditating, trying to release myself from the fear. I imagined I was in the hospital talking to a chaplain. "What," I asked, "do others do before an operation to calm themselves?"

"Oh, that's easy!" he replied, crossing his legs. "They have faith that everything will be fine."

Faith! Faith that I will survive, faith that there will be healing. As I look at Cassie, I know that she will be fine, strong, and full of the future. If I die, she will be filled with sorrow, but the pain will not obliterate her. Whenever she needs me, I will be there. At her elbow with support and love, as Solvig has been for me—even in those dark years when I could not remember.

Chapter 9

MISCALCULATION

Daffodils bloom in the field above the farm in the spring. Skunk cabbage and cattails grow in the lower swamp. If you drive the tractor up the lane, across the ridge and down the gas right-of-way, you find trillium and dogtooth violets, wood geranium and Virginian spring beauties. In the summer, the old orchard, planted by Davidson hands over a hundred years ago, grows thick with fruit, sickle pears, early transparents, and Romanos. The pound apples are so big you can make a pie with one. Down the lane, scattered between poison ivy, are plump thimbleberry and black cap raspberries, dewberries, and tart trailing blackberries. Elderberry grows down the hill, chokecherries proliferate, and concord grapes hang in the front yard. In the evening, a groundhog comes out of his burrow under the tulip tree and sits motionless; the fur around his neck glows softly in the setting sun.

☙❧

When my parents returned to the States from Istanbul in 1962, they made a small but fatal miscalculation. My mother had been offered a job at the State College in Oneonta, but my stepfather had not found a job. They decided that she would set up a home for the family in central New York. He would relocate to the old Davidson family farmhouse just outside of Pittsburgh. While renovating it for rental, he would apply for teaching positions in the Oneonta area. They would live apart for only a year and commute on weekends.

They checked the map; the distance between the two locations was about an inch. Later they realized the map was of the entire United States. The inch turned out to be an eight-hundred-mile round trip. They did not live together again for over forty-five years.

Oneonta, nicknamed the City of the Hills, sits in the northern foothills of the Catskill Mountains between Binghamton and Albany. My mother bought a house on Main Street near the hospital, just walking distance to the grocery store. The plain house was built of white brick, with chestnut paneling and sliding doors. The rooms were small and dark, covered with drab flowered wallpaper. The previous owner had died, and the family sold the house with all its contents. Piles of old clothing, cracked china, and tins of odds and ends, as well as a large collection of sample red lipstick, were like Christmas in September for me. I happily packed box after box of small porcelain statues, old books, and heavy vases to store in the attic. We gave away the long ornamental sword.

By fall we were settled into school and the routine of going down to Pittsburgh every other weekend. On Friday afternoon, my mother rushed home after teaching to pack the car with food and bedding for the eight-hour trip. Leaving shortly after school got out, she drove us down to Binghamton and over to Pennsylvania.

I was in charge of Eva and Scott, and later Lâle and Loren. Scott was like a baby Hercules, strong and fast. Always climbing and running out of the room, Scott was still only when he slept. In the car he struggled. He wanted to drive, he wanted to flip over the seat, he wanted to sit on Mom's lap, he wanted to open the window and lean out. After an hour, my mother's exhausted voice begged, "Sing to him, Tina!"

Holding his damp, chubby two-year-old body close to me, I sang all the songs I knew: several of the Gilbert and Sullivan operettas, Benjamin Britten's *The Little Sweep*, *West Side Story*, *Oklahoma!*, *South Pacific*, and Bible songs, and later all the folk songs of Joan Baez. I sang for hours until it was dark. We fell asleep in a sweaty damp mass in the back seat while my mother drove past Tyrone to Altoona, down the twisty-turnies, arriving in Monroeville late at night. I woke to my stepfather lifting my siblings out of the car. The crickets jazzed, the scent of newly mowed grass hung heavy in the air.

The farmhouse, shaded by tall locust trees, was built by the Davidson family shortly after the Revolutionary War as a two-story, four-room house. Later the house was expanded, doubling the rooms to eight. It was tiny for the seven of us. The thick exterior walls were soft yellow sandstone, the windows deeply recessed. The hand-hewn floor joists were exposed, and constant washing wore the wooden floors to a soft gray. My parents slept in one of the two bedrooms; we children slept in the other and in the hallway. In the summer we pulled our mattresses out on the second-floor porch. The floors sagged, the well water often smelled, and the outhouse listed to one side.

The first year of commuting turned into years of commuting. The renovations to the house went slowly, and my stepfather landed a job teaching at the University of Pittsburgh and then at Duquesne University. My mother was busy with her full-time professor position and now five children. Their lives became separate. We went down to Pittsburgh on a regular basis, but clearly my stepfather was not moving up to Oneonta anytime soon.

Summers were spent together at the farm. The day was always bright with adventure after chores around the house and in the garden were complete. My parents bought us a small red pony named Satan who had foundered gorging on apples in the orchard; his hooves curved up like the slippers of an Arabian prince. Solid and square, his innocuous shape gave lie to his true personality; he was sneaky and mean. Watching out of the corner of his eye, he leaned nonchalantly, casually stretching his neck. Then whipping his head around, he bared his teeth and bit. One morning he took out the whole front of Eva's new Sunday dress.

I loved to saddle him up or ride him bareback the way one rides a bike. We trotted up the lane, brushing past the arched canes of berries, through the orchard to the bony dump, where years of strip mining had left the land open and scarred, covered with a trail of red and white crushed gravel. In the evenings, I tied him out to a stake in the fields and brought him carrots and sugar cubes.

One Easter, my stepfather came home with six soft, downy chicks. Mine was yellow with a black feather on the left wing. We built a small cage and kept them on the side table in the kitchen. My mother was disgusted; he hooted, "City girl!" Soon their soft, round features elongated, and they became quarrelsome, leggy adolescents. In early summer he let them roam the yard and built a large coop up the hill.

Cockerel and Henny-Penny were gentle and almost tame, but my chick, now a full-fledged rooster, was quickly renamed Bully-pecker. Lurking quietly behind a bush or under the front porch, he'd rush out flapping and shrieking to peck at our legs.

We armed ourselves against the terrorist advances of the rooster. Keeping a pail of soft apples from the orchard near the side door and a broom handy, we carefully came out of the house. We'd catch sight of his beady red eye, and stone him with fruit. He retreated indignantly, squawking. One day he flew up and bit my baby sister in the face. My mother put her foot down. Bully-pecker and one of the other roosters became a tough, unhappy meal.

Early on, my stepfather decided to build an addition to the farm so that we could live there comfortably. He consulted an architect and drew up plans that would double the square footage of the house with the same thick sandstone walls and deep window seats. He would build it himself, as his ancestors had, stone by stone, learning as he went. He scavenged the countryside, taking down old houses for the wood and beams. He collected sandstone from barn foundations.

The summer I was thirteen, he was ready to begin. My mother taught summer school up in Oneonta and was away most of the time. A babysitter came in to care for the younger kids. I was excited to become my stepfather's right-hand man.

He had deep trenches cut with a backhoe. Instead of pouring the footer first and the foundation later, he decided to do both together. He set the forms a foot off the floor of the trenches, using the space below as the footer. I helped him build the large plywood forms and crawled down the damp channels, threading the wires to hold the rebar and J-hooks in place.

The work was slower than expected. The weather was terrible and rained almost every day. I spent mornings ankle-deep in water, bailing. Towering over me, he swore under his breath. He was often irritable. He barked out orders or was silent for hours at a time. I nervously tried to anticipate his next command, jumping up before he spoke to get a tool. My body was continually tense. "God damn," he muttered, looking at the work I just completed, his hands on his hips. "God damnit to hell," and ripped out the bent nails, hammering them back straight.

"I don't think he likes me very much," I whispered to my mother on the phone.

"Don't be silly!" she countered. "Of course he loves you!"

Finally the forms were complete and the foundation ready to pour. One late August morning misted with a fine rain; the cement trucks waited to set their chutes. The men huddled with my stepfather, talking about the pour. Then, with a shout of laughter, the work began.

Soon, there was trouble; the footer had widened with the rains and ate up the cement. Several more trucks were ordered. Some of the forms began to buckle and ooze; my father ordered another truck. The day was long. For weeks I wore my war wounds with pride. My fingertips were pitted from the caustic material of the cement; the palms of my hands were like sandpaper.

The next summer, without a word, my stepfather replaced me with my brother Scott. I was relegated inside to cook, clean, and take care of my younger siblings, never again called to help him out in the building of the wing. The little space that had been open the summer before, closed. As I look back at it now, it was the hope that he would, someday, see me. Instead, his gaze continued to move around me or past me.

After the cornerstone was put in place, the wing sat untouched for several years. A stone mason was hired, and slowly the sixteen-inch-deep walls took shape. The roof was not put on for fifteen years; the second floor was completed several years after that. The windows, including a large bay window, purchased early on, sat in the field for decades covered with plastic, infested with mud wasps. Finally the dormers were cut out and the windows set. The fireplace and chimney were completed recently.

Some people are married to their families, some to their work; my stepfather was married to the web of the past. He had an innate love of the ancestral land he owned. Each summer he put on his work boots to preserve the house, planting trees with care, tending the fields above the house faithfully. In the long winters, he researched family history. Scouring flea markets, he created a large collection of primitive American tools: braces, wooden spokeshaves, draw knives, axes, chisels, gouges and slicks, levels, plumb bobs, squares, angle dividers,

marking gauges, trammels, rules, wrenches, and hammers. He gathered hundreds of wooden planes: tongue and groove planes, toted boxwood plow planes, jointer planes, side rebate planes, rosewood coffin smoothing planes, dovetail, grooving, and rabbet planes. Each he carefully wrapped in brown paper and stored away. Shelf after shelf, they sat in the attic.

We went along with the story we created about him. Heroic, solitary, and Whitmanesque in stature, he was in love with the hubbub of life. He joined the land and preserved our place in the ancestral flow of the past. But slowly, the facade gave way to a painful truth; he loved history more than he loved those soft bodies around him. In the narrowness of his vision, he dropped the real jewels of life—his relationship with us. As the grip of the past grew, he became silent, withdrawn, and brooding.

The farm now stands empty; the wing is unfinished. The stately locust trees are gone. The apple and pear trees bear only a small amount of fruit. The lane is overgrown and almost impassable. But in the spring, daffodils bloom by the thousands, their yellow and white heads cascade in the wind.

Chapter 10

HEALING

Philadelphia (1991)

Drinking a cup of tea, I stop the war.
Paul Reps

January 2

The days are long and warm. Wood, Cassie, and I camp at the Long Key State Park with my parents in Florida. The ocean is calm, washing lazily up on the coral reefs. The beach is covered with strands of brown seaweed. This morning the sun rose as the moon set. My husband and I walk down the curve of the beach, looking for shells. Cassie dances ahead. I feel life, I feel the music stirring.

I take off my shirt periodically and look at my scar. Long and bright red, I trace the length with my finger, feeling the small patches of shiny scar tissue. Will I be able to run or bicycle now? Will I be able to stay out without having to rest the next day? Can I jump up and walk to the store without worrying I will be too tired to tend to my family that evening? Can I go to concerts, meetings, out of town conferences?

I feel the weight of the terrible carefulness of the last nine years, where normal living ran me to exhaustion.

January 8

The operation came and went, an event unto itself; it was easier and more difficult than I expected. The physical pain was less than I imagined, but the recovery was arduous, with many difficult days of emotional fragility.

My husband and I flew to Cleveland the day before the operation. After doing research, we had found only two doctors in the country who do mitral valve repair instead of valve replacement. Dr. Delos (Toby) Cosgrove at the Cleveland Clinic agreed to do the operation.

We met him for the first time in the evening before the operation, and I liked him immediately. Dr. Cosgrove, a tall attractive man with enormous hands and a loose lankiness, folded himself down into the chair like a carpenter's ruler. "Are you ready?" he asked with intensity and ease.

The next morning, he brushed into the pre-op room, trailed by his cardiac fellows. They would try to do a repair instead of a replacement, but wouldn't know until they opened me up, he told me. "We might have to strengthen the valve with denatured bull pericardium," he added. Then he was gone in a blur of white.

I blinked. "Does he rip the pericardium with his teeth?" I teased the young doctors. They hesitated. It was early and they were not used to humor.

Then they beamed. "How did you know?"

Previously, I thought I wanted a doctor with a good bedside manner, who listened to me carefully. That morning, however, I was grateful to know that Dr. Cosgrove had performed my procedure so many times that he could do it on a bad day, in his sleep, or half dead on his feet. Every disaster had been faced and solved a hundred times over.

Open-heart surgery, while routine, is no small matter. They saw open your chest, lift aside your lungs, redirect your entire blood flow across the room to the heart-lung machine, cooling it to keep your brain intact. They stop your heart. They cut, repair, and make fine seamstress stitches. A jolt of electricity and they wait quietly for the heart to restart. Then they put your body together again.

The details after the morning preparations for the surgery have dissolved; the kindness remains. The operating room was cool, neat, and orderly. Soft eyes looked at me over masks. Hands lifted me carefully onto a slender hip-wide table covered with a soft, warmed sheep skin. Crisp, heavy blue cotton sheets were spread over me. "What music did you bring?" the nurse asked, gently pulling the cassette tape out of my hands. *Fraters* and *Tabula Rasa* by Arvo Pärt were among the selections. They tugged at my neck, placing in the central venous catheter, and it was dark.

I woke hours later in the dim and dusky ICU to the soft bands around my wrists tying me down. Agitated while coming out of anesthesia, I flailed around. The male nurse bent over me. He pressed a pencil and paper into my hand. *Repair?* I wrote.

"Yes, a repair." All is well. Blessed darkness, sweet rest.

"Wake up, Tina!" the nurse called to me and put his tape player on my chest so I could hear my music. "Wake up!" he shook me gently, getting me to be alert enough to take me off the respirator. My voice croaked. My husband gently washed my feet. Wonderful coolness and relief.

For the next three days there was pain, but also morphine, Darvon, then Motrin. The coughing and walking, the tubes being pulled out, and the strange time distortions passed. All the while, the love of friends and family circled, held, and healed me. When we returned home, dinners awaited us, calls and visits—it was beyond words.

January 10

Grace is a state of balance, a knowledge of things in the past and future, all in accord with the present. Children teach us grace; they are the sweetness and hopefulness of life. And with hope, both the past (dashed hopes) and the future (forbidden dreams) are available. They extend like a giant scale, with me, a fulcrum, in the middle.

January 22

What is it? I am looking for an understanding. I pick up Stephen Levine again.

"Cancer was your teacher for a long time, and perhaps you feel a kind of grief at your teacher leaving. But you don't need that teacher, or that teaching any longer. Cancer isn't the path. You are the path."[1]

My illness has given me knowledge, clarity, and connectedness. My illness protected me against a fast, whirling life. My illness made choices for me so I could function. Now free of illness, I hesitate and hang back. I teeter on the edge of going forward.

I am afraid of the pulse and pace of the future. I slumbered years in my work, an isolated pleasure. I fear the emergence. I am terrified that this new life will devour me and possess me in a way that I will no longer be who I am.

Who and what am I? If I give up the old label of "heart patient," how will I protect and care for myself? If I give up my carefulness and live in hope, will this illness creep back on me like divine retribution?

I need the perspective of time to rest and think, to evolve. There is still the grief for those years of illness, not ever lost, but isolated in the sequestered lonely comfort to reckon with. Like a butterfly, I sit on my chrysalis, drying my still moist, soft wings, grieving the loss of my caterpillar life. My illness will fall off me, and in time, I will let my teacher go.

"We are so identified with the mind/body that we often mistake symptoms of illness for who we are."[2]

January 24

The Gulf War rages. I am heartbroken at the lives lost with the invasion of Kuwait and aerial bombardment.

"Drinking a cup of tea, I stop the war." Love redeems the old law and puts words into action.

loving, I stop the war
being, I stop the war
speaking out, I stop the war
writing music, I stop the war
healing, I stop the war

January 30

I am beginning to read, think, and hear again, with intensity and absorption. Ideas for new works flood me. They are about slow transformation, evolving movements and colors, arrivals that are also departures—being stationary and moving at the same time. I hear a long piece—forty minutes or more for orchestra. A lifetime work, without separation of movements—a continual flow of being.

I move toward the core of my being, into the currents and continuous motion of all things. Just as I finally come to one understanding, another journey begins. The moment is a clearness of rhythms and harmonies and an immense opening up that hangs without motion—gliding on the air currents, effortless and calm.

The journey of my music has always been to find my original face. The deeper I dig, the more upward I move. The more layers I peel back, the broader I become. As I reclaim each stratum, my music grows vertically and horizontally, pushing out, expanding from the center point—a gate-note—one pitch through which my music must go. I envision it as a procession of priestesses walking slowly together through the gate of the temple. They separate at the altar.

The melody is solemn and soaring, opening to the rhythms of life with bumpy, jolting turns and fast changes. The tension increases and suddenly there is a clear point, an opening—the exhilaration of a beautiful sunset, the catch in your throat. Colors whirl and beauty holds us quietly. Finally the emanations whisper, the filaments remain. The rustlings ebb off into the silence.

February 5

I have pink cheeks! I have lived so many years with pallor and without knowing healthy-looking skin. Even before the initial endocarditis infection, did I suffer from cardiac insufficiency? It is like being born.

I have found the poet Rilke.

February 10
The days are warm and beautiful. I hang back, not quite ready to start the new piece. I don't quite understand something.

I am writing a piece for narrator and orchestra for the Greater Twin Cities Youth Symphonies. I will use a story that comes out of the myths of seals, or *selkies,* who are shape changers, able to cast off their selkie skin and become human.

Willie, a little boy, is found on the beach of the Orkney Islands and adopted by a large Scottish family. Somehow he never feels like he belongs and longs for the sea. Little by little he learns about the seals and his true identity.

He finds himself, the way we all must, through tears that reclaim memory. They are the water of life and reconnect him, but not in a flash or a burst of understanding, or even at the top of a primal scream. His memories are disembodied, his dreams whisper and hiss. Guided by child intuition, he weeps—*seven tears dropped, plip, plop, into the water.*[3] They are crystalline, full of eddies and currents. They transport him to his true self and unite him with both his female and male self.

"Compassion is the awakening of the heart."[4]

February 20
Salman Rushdie's new book, *Haroon and the Sea of Stories,*[5] is a wonderful tale written for his son. Rashi, who lost his gift of storytelling, must go to the Coves of Stories to fight against the dark

threat of silence. The story is an allegory about Iran, the curtain of silence, and death of words.

Even though Rushdie's audience is children, his story is rich and complex. He relaxes the structure and language while keeping clarity and a sense of swiftness. Moving his story on gracefully, abounding with humorous tongue-in-cheek language, he is clear on the morality of good and evil. The story glides seamlessly on an inner rhythm and movement, like a burbling stream—the gaiety and forward motion never betrays itself in adult preoccupation or complications. The lack of self-absorption allows for the intricacies of the stories to be all the more visible.

As I start to work on *The Selkie Boy*, I, too, soften my adult perceptions and let the story fall from my mouth. I need not diminish the music, only get to the essence of the story, which is both straightforward and profound.

February 25
I listen today, again, to John Lennon's tender song, "Beautiful Boy."

February 26
"Bairn, bairn," said his mother, for she it was. "We've waited long and long for you. We've seen you on the ebb and upon the rocks and never a word could we say, till you found out who you were."

"Bairn, bairn," said his father, for he it was. "Can't you find a Selkie skin and come back to your own folk?"

And he ran to the sea and dove from his rock, with his Selkie skin about him, while the sun played music on the dimpled water and the Selkie folk turned and twisted in glee to meet him."[6]

February 27

I am haunted by a dream that I was to have open-heart surgery all over again. There is a slight imperfection that remains in my valve, a redundancy and motion in the wall. I am in the hospital, waiting, afraid to question their decision. I phone Dr. Cosgrove. Immediately he walks into the hospital room, and we sit side by side on the bed and talk. "This is not the time," he finally says. "Wait." We walk out of the hospital together.

Since my operation, my surgeon has become a larger-than-life person. He, through kindness and excellence, restored me to life. I imagine him to be good, decent, and honorable. In the way that one falls temporarily in love with one's psychiatrist, I am in love with my healer.

He is boyish and young in my dream. He sits next to me like a sibling, snuggled up against the pillows, his shoulder touching mine. "Wait," he says. Life does not have to be perfect to be healed. The heart can have its imperfections and still claim life.

I struggle to lay title to my new life. Rather like claiming joy and love after being in pain. Does the victim ever put the rape behind her? Does the beaten man ever walk with the old confidence in his step? Does the sexually abused child ever find love and contentment in intimate connection?

Trust is difficult to hang on to. Intellectually, I know it is possible to live with the memory of pain and loss in love and joy, and—perhaps most precariously—in hope or faith. Belief in the better nature of people. But right now, I can't hold on. Trust slips from my hands.

In my dream, Dr. Cosgrove bends over and picks it up for me; I trust through his proxy. However the means, wonderfully enough, here I am. This is truly grace.

Grace just is. There is no explanation or rationale for it. As many times as I have misplaced it or forgotten it existed, there it is again—a light, calm, and a relaxing of body and spirit. "Ah," my body breathes. "Ah," my spirit sighs.

Grace is the grand release. Grace is understanding beyond knowledge. Grace is peace and calm. Grace is stillness and movement. It is the moment after the music has ended but still continues. The audience leans forward to catch what is not there. It has ended, but it has not. And that sound, that movement, that evanescence hangs in the air for a moment that transcends time.

Grace is all of life in a moment, a moment of supreme understanding, complete surrender and satisfaction.

March 5

I grow disconnected as the time nears to make the final step in my next piece. The material is written, a ciphery of note heads strewn over many smudged pages. I have the whole in my hand almost like an architectural drawing—without real substance until the first brick is laid. Soon it will be time to put the notes in place between bar lines.

I am restless and irritable. I pace and growl, find other things to do, and waste time. I want to move forward and to stay back simultaneously. I am dissatisfied. I will never get ahead, never have the commissions and performances I need. Others are moving up on the ladder, up the road, up the stretch, while I lag. Discontent follows me everywhere.

I am so predictable! This always happens as I start to write.

March 15

Rushdie said: "There are two aesthetic lessons. Unfortunately, they contradict each other. One is that one must place clarity above all other virtues in a work of art. If the work is capable of being misread or misunderstood, it is the artist's fault. The other lesson is: it is impossible to learn from what other people think of your work. All you can do is write the books that are in you to write. And sometimes you'll be right and sometimes you'll be wrong."[7]

March 16

I stay up late thinking. It has been a long time since I have had the energy to do this.

What is life's work? Does everyone have a thing waiting to be fulfilled?

I understand life's work as what is meant to be. It transforms in a reciprocal fashion—as I do life's work, I am transformed and so is the work. Both breathe together as one. Life's work is all sides of things: wonderful, painful, demanding, rewarding, one's great joy, and one's most terrible burden. Intrinsic is a certain humbleness, even supplication. I yield to the work, usually after a long resistance. I am small before it and relax, lie bare before it. A calm, cool energy flows back and forth, a gentle rocking of understanding.

I know nothing about purpose or divine plan; it seems simplistic and patriarchal. But I feel a magnetic force that pulls each of us. I can either resist or yield.

April 1

The well-known string quartet played my piece *I Hear the Mermaids Singing,* which I had recently rescored for the ensemble.

When they are not playing European complexities (music), they sound quite wonderful and did a great job with my piece.

They, like many string quartets, are their own enigma. The first violinist is small and quick, classic in his lean and aggressive sound; a superb musician pursued by an ego. The second violinist's round sound is like his round body. He is smart and deeply knowledgeable about contemporary literature. The violist is lovely and leans into the low notes of the viola. The cellist is haunted by melancholy. His playing is vital and quick, but during the luncheon he lapses into a long silence, a sweet mournfulness.

I have no idea how the quartet manages to share the day together, rehearsing and performing. I am solitary enough that the idea of being part of a group is curious and unfathomable.

April 18
I am excited to be writing an article about women composers for *Ms.* magazine for publication next year. At hand is gender and music and how I celebrate myself as a voice that includes my femaleness and sexuality.

For instance, what is sexual energy in music? In classical music the climax (don't you love the nomenclature?) is the culmination of rhythmic and harmonic tension. The climax arrives in a pumping, stumping, squirting fashion, collapsing into a kind of stewed silence. Now I ask you, is that me? (okay, perhaps sometimes).

But truthfully, my sexuality seems dark and powerful. It comes out of a center place and is wide, continuous, warm, moist. My physical energy is long and deeply rooted.

It goes on and on, winding from one rhythm to another slowly moving out, until at its peak it is suddenly transformed into something else – a glowing, evanescing energy. This, for me, is not a climax, but an epiphany. [8]

April 20
Cassandra looms large as I write this article.

Women composers are singing like Cassandra more than ever these days. They have emerged in the twentieth century from past virtual obscurity to be a vital part of the contemporary new music scene. I know many whose music is strongly identified with their total selves, and yet there are equally as many who harbor a curious doubt and nagging disbelief of the importance of gender.

Listen to this from a well-known, Pulitzer Prize-winning woman composer: "Nobody refers to Beethoven as a man composer ... It's obvious that I'm a woman and my womanhood is important to me. But I don't write music as a woman or as a man; I write music as a composer."

These are haunting words, for they begin with a separation of self. If she does not write as a woman, who then does she write as? Who is this composer, this disembodied voice?

May 5
I am engulfed by music lately. The work on the orchestra piece is consuming. The music sits on my brain like a fat frog. I need space from it.

June 26

The work on *The Selkie Boy* is complete. I am released to go off into the blue beyond, off to Wyoming.

I am looking for something. Of course, a break from family problems and interactions (my husband's schedule is all absorbing, and even when he is home he is distant and dark) and time to rest and rejuvenate. But there is something more.

Space. Inside and outside of me. The call is to go West, to open myself up to a sweeping, a rolling, a largeness. To be more than the interior of the past nine years, so confined by illness.

I leave in two days.

June 28

Cody, Wyoming, the first afternoon, is dark and overcast. At night, I cannot see the full moon. But today is blue and so bright; the mountains are clear and tremendous. As I walk, I am reminded of other solitary walks and weeping landscapes—green, green meadows and black-gray skies.

The landscape of the West is hewn instead of molded. There are no soft contours, instead craggy cliffs and sharp gullies. Heart Mountain is off to the west, with the mouth of Yellowstone Park to the north. The Big Horn Mountains, where I will go tomorrow, are to the east, blue and large. And always the wildflowers, delicate and tough.

The new work I am hearing is different. I feel its weight and am reluctant to take up the responsibility. *Bleached Thread, Sister Thread,* commissioned for the Mendelssohn Quartet, takes the title from one of Eva's poems. These are old issues—sister bonds, attachments, and delicate fine stuff—a sense of joy, release, and gratitude.

Gratitude reappears in my mind. I find it difficult to accept gifts without payment. So used to a bad turn, a broken heart, it is almost beyond my understanding to accept the gift of returned health without sacrifice. Pain has always defined me.

Will gratitude now make me one of them? One of whom?

Opening oneself to grace.

June 30

I have joined a week-long pack trip into the Big Horn Mountains. We ride horses for hours up the trail; the saddle creaks, my bones ache, and the horses snort. I chat with the other participants, getting to know them. The wind blows fierce and cold from over the hills. Small blue and yellow flowers are underfoot, and the roll of the hills, the steepness of the rock, is breathtaking. Wyoming is large.

My life has lacked this expanse. In the years of illness, the view has only been out of my studio window. I have always had distance within me; I have not had it without. Here the openness is incredible. The vistas fill me up and out, stretching beyond present imagination. "I am large, I contain multitudes," says my dear friend, poet Walt Whitman.

It comes on me so fast I can hardly breathe. I understand what it is I must do. Now is a time of harvest, a time of bringing in the fruit of years of toil, of accepting the promise, not of tomorrow, but of today.

Each day I find a gift. Today, a pine cone with delicately shaped seeds all set to fly away.

July 2

The weather turns moody and showers sporadically. We climb one of the ridges by the stream, going from one rock to another. Near the top, one of the group suddenly gives out. She sits there, shoulders hunched. They discuss endlessly if they should return to camp. I have little patience for the talk and keep my distance.

I wander up the steep incline, and eventually a guide comes after me. We reach the top—the fruit—a beautiful view of the valley and the mountain range beyond. I see them in my mind's eye, dancing in the distance.

The next day we ride on horseback to the medicine wheel. The day is cold with brisk winds, and it takes several hours to ascend to eleven thousand feet or more. We ride up the steep hills and across the meadows of blue forget-me-nots. White and pink flowers, the sun in our face, the breath knocked out of our bodies. On a plateau, the view of split, weathered rocks crumbling off into nothing stands before us. Far below, dark green meadow and trees are moist and delicious. A sky-blue bird, slender and delicate, flies among the rocks.

The medicine wheel itself is, at first, unremarkable looking. Flat rocks seem tossed in a circle; a fence enclosed the grounds. I sit quietly for some time; the ground is surely sacred and profound. I leave a heart-shaped stone I had found the day before, an offering in gratitude for the return of health.

July 6

We climb the mountain on the other side of the stream. It is steep; we stop and rest often. Near the top, we eat carrots and talk. A fraternity of sorts, a camaraderie.

Illness made small distances seem immense. A walk to the mailbox was a day's work, standing to cook dinner sent me to bed. Even social interaction—talking, sharing—depleted. What pleasure it is to have the energy to climb the hill and listen to friends!

July 10

Home again, I sit in my studio. What is it that I must compose? It is the time to explore my newly expanded body and soul.

The Wyoming trip was a re-initiation into life. Each day brought me new understandings. First, it is a time of harvest and opening up. Second, a return of trust in my body; I am quick and strong. Third, acceptance of grace and return of health without payment. Fourth, companionship. Fifth, reliance on others. And sixth, my healed body has its limits!

The trip allowed me to internalize a breathless view of the world. The mountains and plains affirm both the known and unknown. I learn to fly when offered spaciousness, to breathe when provided sweet air and cold wind, and to trust the natural suppleness and energy when offered a challenge.

My body, confined by illness, gave my heart time and space to grow. The healed heart now gives my core a chance to expand beyond its physical dimension.

As I look into the hills, I become the hills, the rolling green, the far-off, white-covered peaks. They lie crisp and clean in the distance. Each cell of my body, each hair on my skin stretches out and becomes wide, rolling, craggy, deep, and tall from horizon to horizon.

July 15
I begin to hear *Bleached Thread, Sister Thread* for the Mendelssohn String Quartet. This piece is about blessings, gratitude for the return to a whole body and heart. Quietly and with bursts of light, a song emerges out of rubbing—a soft shuddering.

> *what was gathered or what was learned;*
> *and now you and I will tell each other*
> *what we know, that to be distant*
> *is sometimes closer than to be near.*[10]

August 2
Summer has ended early down at the shore. The house is rented, and we will spend time instead with various friends. I dreamed last night I was teaching at college. I awake longing for Bennington College.

August 9
These are the bitter days of our marriage. I try not to spill out on my husband, who is dispirited. His life is in a tumble. Never has it been so difficult to love him or be with him. I am filled with loneliness and frustration. The return to health has not given our marriage new energy as I had hoped.

September 1
Things have burst open. Amid the difficulty, there is clarity. I am no longer willing to live like this with him. I weep daily.

September 16
The shape of *Bleached Thread* keeps changing. In this piece, I am guided more by the material than the form. There is a black energy in my stomach. Despite the clear, calm weather, the days are unsure.

September 18
Material for the string quartet is finished. It came on its own accord.

At first I was conflicted over the work moving in a direction I had not planned. But when I view the construction with curiosity instead of tension, the work reveals itself. The energy of the music is fierce in its optimism, constantly moving forward and changing. I feel the animation of health restored, of a future fullness refreshed.

Yet, still, still—a disconnection. Despite the celebration, a fracture in my life shows itself. The piece ends in a deep sadness. I cannot control this; I only allow what is.

October 4
Days are warm after the cool end of last month. The work on the quartet goes well. Sometimes I panic and think the material is thin or the movement static. The next day, however, I like the sparseness; the movement waxes fuller and fuller rather than moving directionally.

I have lunch with composer Bernard Rands, currently serving as composer-in-residence with the Philadelphia Orchestra. In his mid-fifties, he has white hair and an interesting face. Dressed in black corduroys and a pinstripe shirt, he sits with his glasses dangling around his neck—a combination of impressive and endearing. Genteel and collegiate, he is perfect for the world of the Philadelphia Orchestra.

I am, at times, jealous of other composers' opportunities. But as we lunch on food and wine, I see how well suited he is to be this orchestra's composer, and how I am not. I am too raw and often not well-mannered.

November 10
The late autumn weather continues. I am calm, yet not always certain. Slowly I make plans. The future becomes clear and focused.

November 18
Cassie brought down an old photograph of my husband and me. We, in our beginning years, smile warmly, our arms around each other. My long hair blows up into his young, brown face, our heads tilt toward each other. She cradles the frame and takes it to school for Show and Tell. She must know without knowing.

Our time continues quiet and without interruption. I wait for Cassie's birthday, Thanksgiving, and Christmas. Then my husband and I will move on. One moment I feel a terrible sadness, the next ambivalence.

The day is cold and sunny; we plant bulbs and shop for Cassie's birthday. Wood sings snatches of songs as he cooks dinner. His voice is sweetly thin and out of tune. I read to Cassie in the growing darkness of the evening. It is a good day.

December 20
I take Cassie up to my mother's for Christmas. When we return, we will tell her together that the marriage is over.

The new chapter begins. I am alternately terrified and calm about the loneliness and responsibility, Cassie's future anger and sadness, and how I will make a living. I keep in front of me the possibility that I will have something different in my life than I have now, something other.

Chapter 11

COOL WATERS

The morning is still dark as I creep down the stairs. I am five, and under the Christmas tree are two boxed sets of LPs—Gilbert and Sullivan's Mikado *and* The Pirates of Penzance. *I finger the cardboard, open the lid, and feel the weight of the four black disks in each box. My small phonograph is blue and silver with a hinged cover. I sit on the floor and open it carefully. Slipping the record out of its sleeve, I put it on the turntable. Holding my breath, I lower the arm onto the disk. The needle sinks into the shiny grooves of plastic. I lose myself in the scritch scratch of the margin. I wait for the music to fill me.*

∽✞∾

While the farm in Pittsburgh was sunny and spacious, the house in Oneonta, where we spent the remaining nine months, was cramped, noisy, and chaotic. My mother, out of the house teaching, left the bulk of the childcare to my grandmother, who now lived with us full-time. Her small frame and arthritic twisted back, however, did not give her much weight. As she aged, her walk was

133

reduced to a shuffle, and her thin voice was full of criticism. Eva hid in her bedroom, the downstairs was littered with toys, and Scott, trailed by Lâle, was either on the cusp of an adventure or exploding with frustration.

School, for me, was not much better. After three years in Istanbul, I did not fit in. I was awkward and often outspoken. The girls wore saddle shoes with white socks and had knee-length petticoats under flared skirts. Too young for beehives, they wore their hair in a bouffant, teased and sprayed. My long flyaway hair was out of style, and worse, I defended spiders and thought communism was interesting. Quickly I was nicknamed "Tina-white-legs," "witch," and "turkey." I had no friends and sank into my own world of music and books.

My mother started me on the piano when I was five, and by the time I was seven I was practicing an hour a day. She coaxed me with an allowance of five cents an hour, which I renegotiated sometime later to ten cents. By the time we landed in Oneonta I was a fairly good pianist.

My piano teacher, Mr. Wolman, was a patient, kind man with thick dark-framed glasses and slicked-down hair. He taught at the state college and was a middle-aged solitary bachelor. The music he gave me was unusual and often contemporary: Persichetti, Bartok, Villa-Lobos, Octavio Pinto, Ibert, Debussy, and William Schuman. Sometimes I practiced, but often I did not. I was in love with books.

The local library, housed in a converted Victorian home, was at the other end of town. On fall afternoons, I biked over with my books piled up in the front basket. The crisp yellow cotton of my pedal pushers flashed as I went past Wilbur Bank, across the parking lot, behind Breese Department Store, and up a small hill to the library. The door was stiff and heavy, and once inside, life was muffled and circumspect. Soft voices murmured as patrons checked books out, and feet weighted the floorboards carefully.

At the time, I was reading a series of biographies. Annie Oakley, Helen Keller, Florence Nightingale, and Molly Pitcher (Girl Patriot) were my heroes. The library allowed me to check out ten books a week, so I assumed that I *had* to read each book. All day, I lounged, curled on the chair in the study, sprawled on the living room floor, face down on the top bunk bed late by the hallway light. Falling asleep, I put my book under the mattress and reached for it first thing upon waking. Reading was a safe haven, where I could imagine myself without restrictions, where I could blot out my surroundings.

One week I decided I would combine reading with my practicing. It seemed like an efficient, thrifty thing to do. While my mother prepared dinner, I sat in the dark living room at the Chickering upright she had gotten for free. The piano was enormous and sat like an overstuffed chair in the corner of the room. The cracked keys had long ago sunk into the frame, and the circular piano stool creaked and rocked. Placing my novel carefully on the rack, I began to practice from memory while I read. Oblivious to many of the details of her children, my mother didn't notice as I stumbled through the music. She called out encouraging remarks from the kitchen.

My piano teacher wasn't as easy to fool. At my lesson, he opened the first piece I was learning. There was no obvious progress. He closed the music without comment. He opened the next piece with similar result. Five minutes in on the hour-long lesson,

I slumped at the piano. He picked up his car keys. "I'll drive you home," he said quietly. I sat in his car dazed, and once home, wept in the easy chair in the corner of the dining room. I had betrayed his kindness and interest; worse, the lessons were expensive, my mother reminded me often, and I had wasted her money.

She was careful with expenses, noting each in a small note-book she kept stashed in her purse. She portioned out every-thing—one pork chop, one slice of cake for each of us. There were no second helpings or leftovers. "You've had your share," my grandmother warned. While the fruit bowl was always full, there never seemed to be enough.

My mother was present as much as she was absent. She was interested in big feelings—Hamlet's hatred or Anna Karenina's tragic fate—not focused on the small emotional hurts of children. She molded us, naming us. "Eva," she often said, "is the artistic talent in the family, and Scott is the genius."

I was, I suspected, ballast. When my little sister was born, she took me aside to explain. "Now we each have a baby! Eva is mine, Scott is Dad's, and Lâle is yours!" I swelled with pleasure. I was needed. When she felt faint at the sight of blood, I learned the art of infirmary nurse, and when she was too tired to bathe the children at night, I leaned over the big blue bathtub downstairs and later wiped up splashed water.

My mother was her best when she was talking or teaching. She read faithfully every night to us for an hour or more; I heard *Gulliver's Travels* and *Great Expectations* before I was seven. A trip to the museum was hours of listening to her tell stories of myths and legends. The long car rides down to Pittsburgh were filled with plots of novels.

Her interest in the arts was broad and inclusive. She played violin with the local orchestra, and I went to all their concerts. Avid about the theater, she took me to college productions of Ibsen, Chekhov, Miller, and Wilde. When the musical films of Jeanette MacDonald and Nelson Eddy were showing at the local movie theater, she had me go. And when composer John Cage and dancer-choreographer Merce Cunningham came to the college for a week residency, she arranged for me to leave my sixth-grade class and walk across the school playground to the open rehearsals in Old Main.

I was, by then, in love with dance. I read about early ballerinas—Marie Taglioni, Fanny Elssler, and Carlotta Grisi. I had steeped myself in Diaghilev's Ballets Russes and the great dancers Vaslav Nijinsky and Anna Pavlova. I clipped magazine articles about Rudolf Nureyev and Margot Fonteyn, following their every move. But I knew almost nothing about modern dance or electronic music.

There was a hush when I entered the darkened auditorium. Dancers in leggings and sweatshirts sprawled on the stage, stretching in the dim lights. I walked past John Cage and David Tudor setting up their equipment to sit in the front. Stage lights came on and off, and a disembodied voice called down from high. Finally, the main spotlight came on, and Merce Cunningham walked slowly into the light. Dressed in white tights and leotard, he rippled like a cat, his fawn-like face large and luminous. I only remember the deliberate, beautiful motions, the quietness and grace.

Merce Cunningham opened a door in me to something I could not name. My heart softened and yielded to the purity of movement. There was more out there than I had imagined. I came out into the quiet afternoon forever changed.

My memories of those years in Oneonta are dark with a few occasional moments of light. As early as I can remember, I would lose myself for days, sometimes for months or years. Pulling back from the sharpness of the moment, I slipped into the coolness of a murky lake. The world receded; the water made the downy hairs on my face stand on end. Air escaped from my nose and the bubbles clung to my face. Part survival, part addiction, it is what clinicians describe as dissociation. In the dark parts of my life, I was happy to lie down in the earth and pull the wet leaves over my head. Always a peaceful, cool reprieve from what was around me. The muffled sounds of life were all-absorbing.

Music had the same call, a place of peace. The hidden lake was always smooth. I flew close to the surface, almost touching the water with my body. I turned up in the air, high, into the sky, then dove down to skim the surface again. Hearing became everything, the rush of the wind on my cheeks, the thump of my heart, and the creak of my body.

I was a swoop, a streak of energy. I was pure joy and delight in my own agility. I sank into sound; I am the wind, the rush and the burble. I am the cool water.

Chapter 12

COMING TOGETHER

Philadelphia (1992)

*To hold on to himself and to let go of himself at the same time—
that is the way of the warrior. Thus he embodies the integration
of the receptive and creative, living and loving the paradoxes of
life, balancing both the terror and the wonder of being human.*
Linda Schierse Leonard[1]

January 7

My husband has moved out. The house is oddly quiet. Cassie's
emotions are swift; her face tightens as sadness crosses her face. But
after one week, she announces it is "time to spend a night with
Daddy." I go shopping, take myself to a movie, and sleep with the
dog guarding the night. Sophie, more vigilant than ever, investi-
gates every noise, rushing back to her bed next to mine.

Early this morning I dream there is a battle. I hear a shout:
"Surrender!"

I shout back, "No!"

January 8

Forgiveness keeps coming up. My neighbor Mary and I drink tea
together. Her kitchen is plain and scrubbed down to the wood, a
home of a family devoted to social justice, comfortable but spare.
She works with children who have endured years of physical,

sexual, and emotional abuse. "How can you forgive those who harm children?" she wonders. How do you forgive evil? Can forgiveness restore love or make it safe for these children, especially when harm is done by a family member?

Forgiveness is simply to clean house and remove the hurt from my landscape. I think of my stepfather and his inability to love me in a tangible way. His body parts litter my life like a Dali painting—an arm here, a leg there. I trip and fall over memories, hurting myself again and again.

Forgiveness is the final step where the absolution is mine. I am released from the power of the harm. As I reduce and neutralize him, I keep the gifts he gave me. Hidden under my pain are the love of the earth, strength and flexibility of trees, connectedness to the past, and his broad, strong hands.

February 26

I grapple with the ending of my new piece. Does the energy transform into a still point, or is it unto itself? What is the balance between terror and wonder? What is "sitting there" energy that doesn't change or go anywhere? I only know a deep body sense, but struggle for words.

My energy comes from a center place and expands outward in a kind of fullness without grasping or overwhelming. The energy exists unto and for itself; there is no motive other than being. Like mountains or volcanoes, like the ocean, it is guileless. Wonder without intent. Turn away from these edifices of nature, they continue in memory, persistent, eternal. Lost or misplaced, they are there at the next turn. So simply. Just this much.

March 20

First day of spring is here. This morning we went to Cassie's teacher meeting. Her reading has slipped in the last month, and her ability to cope with disappointments dwindles. She is difficult and easily upset.

April 22

Finally, finally I get to the end of the piece. Instead of oscillating chords, the chords are beaten, overlapping between the two pianos. The sound gives a sense of surrender and release without losing the intensity.

May 15

The week has been long and extremely tiring. The first draft of the new piece is complete, but there are many loose ends.

I put together a draft for the separation agreement between Wood and me.

June 5

The letter, thin and almost transparent, sits in the mailbox. My heart sinks. So many rejections, I think as I open the letter, comforting myself in advance. But there it is, a Pew Fellowship and a grant of $50,000. I sink to the floor of the hallway. Two years without worry, two years to build a good place for myself and Cassie. The work spreads out far in front of me.

"I am the earth, I am the root. I am the stem that feeds the fruit."[2]

June 11

The photographer from the *Philadelphia Inquirer* comes today to take pictures of me in my studio for an article about the Pew Fellowships. I stand in the tall frame of the window with the sun slanting in. Just as the photo shoot ends, Cassie comes running in. "Take a picture of me with Mommy," she laughs. We stand together, a tangle of dresses and bare feet.

The photographer takes his time leaving, looking carefully at the family photos I have on the fireplace. He points to Wood. "What does your husband do?" he asks.

"Medicine," I murmur, not mentioning our separation.

"Ah," he says, "your husband is a doctor! You don't really need the fellowship," he adds as he leaves the room.

July 23

The saxophone concerto is in my ear. The shape has an architectural feel to it—with an entrance and exit. The portal is contained, a devotion, an honoring, as well as forgiveness, so the real blessing of life can be received. The exit is a beginning, life energized and lightened. The saxophone is a voice calling out for a blessing. I call out as well.

July 28

A beautiful, clear, bright, cool day. Cassie sits on an animal swing with four chains in the park, swinging back and forth. The chains creak and scream, high and overlapping, a shrill cry.

I am composing finally. "After two days of ranting and raving, mercy descended."[3]

August 4

I work on the saxophone concerto with earnestness. It is on my mind constantly. I listen, knowing both time and persistence are on my side. Sometimes I have to hear all the old ways first, before I can steer clear to a new place. Always, a balance between movement and patience. If I move too soon, I run over myself. If I relax too much, there is nothing.

I work and wait.

September 1

I focus on the solo, the "first person" of this piece. This is, in many ways, the first flight. Rupture—big glissando section. Out of the disorganization comes the voice. Out of sound come melody and energy. How do I give the saxophone support to improvise without boxing him in?

October 2

New Music Across America Festivals are in the first day. After a year of fundraising with AT&T, Rockefeller Foundation, and Lila Wallace Reader's Digest Foundation, I have managed, advertised, and promoted eighteen festivals of experimental new music—two in Canada, two in Europe, and fourteen across the US. Over a four-day period, new music will resound all across the land.

Ultimately, the festival is a triumph of community building. Like concentric interlocking rings, each ring is vital. Presenters experience that they are not isolated; their work multiplied by eighteen others is substantial. They, in turn, build community in their cities by honoring and celebrating the richness and diversity of their local artists. Finally, composers are brought into the community with each other and with the audience. Each circle is within a circle; one cannot exist without the other. The work is about inclusivity and celebrating life.

Vision, however, as Black Elk[4] reminds me, is only part of the equation. To reveal it to others, not once but over and over again, is the real work. "Where there is no vision, the people shall perish,"[5] Proverbs contends. But, to obtain the power of a vision, it must be shared with the people.

I have no argument with my commitment. But, in the back of my mind, I ask, am I capable enough? Do I have the strength, courage, devotion, and self-discipline? Can I overcome my own self-gratification? Am I willing to transform constantly to serve others? What if I am nothing but a drop in the bucket; will I have the courage to face that I did not make a difference?

Be still, Tina, be still. Everything has to do with you, and nothing to do with you.

Remember the burning bush on Mt. Sinai. We take off our shoes, shield our eyes, and throw ourselves on the ground. The heat is terrible, our skin smokes and burns—it is awe-inspiring. Yes, here we are. This thing, so much, so terrible, so wonderful, is life, and the life of the people.

October 5

The festival is over, and there is a sense of closure and beginning. I look forward to composing more than ever. Because of personal upheaval, I haven't written much, nor have I felt much like writing. The drummers on Saturday night woke my heart to the next piece—full of rhythms and flight, smiles of arrival, and the joy of being.

October 23
Long days with the Rockefeller Foundation, reviewing grant applications for them while Cassie stays with her father. We sit all day in front of scores and listen to recordings of hopeful presenters, performers, and composers. As I read the applications, I am impressed both by how much I know about the new music field and how little.

October 28
My saxophone concerto feels critical to me, and I am not totally prepared for it. This last year I have been *doing* life instead of *being* life, and I have failed to sniff ahead. Gratefully, I have established my own musical vocabulary. I can rely on knowing and speaking of who I am.

Now, I need to put on my work boots and commit time to thinking and experimenting. I will hold off a bit on the product and work to deepen my clarity and focus. At the same time, I want to dance and play, revitalize my deep and abiding commitment to my work.

November 2
Election day tomorrow. I feel excitement about Bill Clinton's election. For the first time in a long time, I have hope for the political future of the country.

November 18
These two and a half days are set aside to be alone, explore, and start. The house down in New Jersey is quiet, empty.

What is it that I seek? I've grown out of my life in a way one grows out of clothes. The clothes are faded and soft, but the shirts are too short, the sleeves tight, ever so slightly uncomfortable. I am vague and disinterested. I look out the window; I want something else.

Winter is the best time to find myself. The cold drives me inward. The wind whips around the house. Red embers glow in the fire at night, and the wood gases sing a strange song. Is this what I must find—a song of myself? I am distracted by nagging thoughts, minor insults, guilt, and worries.

November 19

There has been good work on my piece. The beginning has a metallic howl, the slow-growing melody goes well.

In the afternoon, I walk on the beach. The skies over the ocean are gray; the waves are dark. The wind is so cold that my ears ache. I sit in the sand and watch the overlapping clouds move their layers. A bright spot is in the sky where the sun almost comes through.

The houses on the ocean are boarded up. Like trees without leaves, they are without life. I trudge past them; their eyes are shuttered to winter and the wind.

November 20

Today, the work on this piece discourages; I lose heart and go shopping for Christmas presents. I contemplate a movie. I eat gummy bears, drink coffee, and sigh over a new flannel nightgown. I snarl at smokers.

What am I doing here? I rescheduled my life, bartered for my daughter's care, and skipped my father's important awards ceremony. I listen, think, and still don't know what is supposed to happen in this piece.

In the evening I sit reading by the fire and watch the flames. I turn out the lights and look deep into the heat and sing. I dance. My shadow fills the room.

November 22
In morning's first light, all is not lost. Even my music has possibilities.

November 30
My piece is almost complete. I have a few weeks of orchestrating, and it will be done by the first of the year. The last ten days have been a wonderful slide home. Once I was able to accept the flaws and disappointments of the piece, I started making progress.

December 21
I've cleared my desk.

On Saturday I heard Zakin Hussein and his percussion ensemble. What delight is the camaraderie of drumming! The rhythms are tricky, the performers merge and cascade over each other. Finally, they arrive all in one spot, the rhythms intertwine. Wreaths of smiles shine from their faces, the joy of communion— of coming together.

Chapter 13

PASSPORT

The front door swings open with a soft whoosh. A bicycle wheel tick-ticks as it is brought in. I am huddled in bed on the third floor in my small bedroom. Gusts of air slap the windowpanes. I am studying for my test, memorizing chemistry equations. My fingers are icy.

He has returned, late at night, from the lab. Tiredly, he pulls himself up the stairs with his left hand, the heavy canvas bag full of science articles and grant proposals still to read and edit in the other. He pauses at the landing. I listen. His footsteps turn and he continues up the stairs, down the narrow hallway crammed with bookcases, into my room.

Every evening, like clockwork, he comes to perch on the corner of my bed. We talk no more than five minutes about the day and what I am learning. He stands to kiss me goodnight. His lips pucker; the whiskers of his chin graze my forehead. I watch as he leaves.

I have no idea he is my father.

✺

I was fifteen when my mother suddenly insisted I go away to school in 1968. Oneonta was too depressed, she told me, talking over her shoulder as she graded her students' papers. The local high school was too ordinary; I needed a good education. I dreamed of Interlochen Arts Academy in northern Michigan, wanting nothing more than to play music all day. My mother had other ideas. She enrolled me in Baldwin School, a formidable, private all-girls boarding and day school outside of Philadelphia.

"Britton Chance and his family will look in on you," she informed me. She hesitated and then added, "He is an old friend of the family." I was quiet on the ride down to the school in late August. I had no idea what to expect.

The school was founded in 1888 by Miss Florence Baldwin at a time when it was considered to be foolish, if not reckless, to educate women. The main residence was an old hotel, a five-story, château-style building designed by Frank Furness. The headmistress, Rosamond Cross, greeted us gravely. She was slender, tall, white-haired, and terrifying. Later at dinner, I came down with the other boarders carefully dressed. The dining room was set with white linen, a teacher at each table. In the morning, outfitted in a gray kilt and a white button-down shirt, I walked with the other students to the schoolhouse for my first day. My shoulder was weighed down with a dark blue book bag; my oxfords clicked on the walkway.

I was a fish out of water. Having lazed through school daydreaming, I had no idea how to study. Mrs. Ely's wrinkled and rheumatic fingers pointed out the cosign and tangents, Mrs. Davenport valiantly tried to get me to write a topic sentence, and Mrs. Sauterwaite spoke French with a southern accent that

I could not decipher. In the evenings, doors opened to our hall proctor's gaze. I studied, hopelessly.

My roommate was friendly and kind, but I was aloof and demoralized by the academics. Instead, I hung out with two other girls and played endless games of Hearts in one of the small sunny rooms on the fifth floor. Their maxim, earnestly applied, was "win if you can, lose if you must, but always cheat," and I lost continually. Even the few times I was invited to the Chance family farm or the New Jersey shore for a weekend did not change the bleakness of that year.

That spring, my mother was appointed to direct the college's foreign exchange program, with a visiting professorship in Würzburg, Germany. I was happy to take the year off from Baldwin. My stepfather stayed behind, and the five of us children and my mother left for Europe.

The summer was bright, blue, and warm. We lived in Donaueschingen, a beautiful little town in the Black Forest. We studied German in a six-week intensive program. By September, my mother found a small apartment on the top floor of a private residence a few miles from Würzburg and enrolled my siblings in the local elementary school. I attended the Matthias-Grünewald Gymnasium, a musical high school, and studied piano at the conservatory.

Often, my mother left me in charge when she went to work. I was irritable and solitary, and having to care for the younger four did not improve my disposition. Eva, nine, was thin and bossy; Scott, seven, was always into mischief. Lâle, at five, was still my darling little sister, and Loren was a soft and dimpled two-year-old. When they played quietly, I read or wrote in my journal. But

when they were fighting, disaster broke out. Loren rode his tricycle back and forth in the tiny hallway, dressed as an Indian chief.
Scott threatened to jump out the third-floor window. One day he
cut off all his hair. Frau Michler, our landlady, routinely thumped
a broomstick handle on the ceiling below us to quiet us down.

Soon, I had a boyfriend, and life brightened. Wolfgang was
a senior in school and a wonderful organist. Sporting a blond
afro, he was passionate about Bela Bartok's music and the writing of Max Frisch. Music, no longer academic, flew off the page
and became part of almost every interaction. We sat in his room,
talking about music, books, and art. Late at night, we crept into
his church and, pulling out all the stops, played the organ till the
stained glass windows rattled. I traveled, went to concerts, argued
passionately with friends about politics, and practiced the piano.
By the end of the year, I spoke fluent German and was filled with
my first flush of confidence and ambition.

On our return to the US, my mother accepted an invitation from
the Chance family. I was to live with them for my final year at
Baldwin instead of boarding. They would take good care of me,
she assured me.

The Chances lived in a large duplex Victorian house in West
Philadelphia, with red-flocked wallpaper, parquet floors, and
a Steinway piano in the front high-ceiling parlor. Charismatic,
with silvering hair and dark-rimmed glasses, Britton Chance was
a well-known scientist at the University of Pennsylvania.

Lil, his second wife, was tall and handsome. "Call me Ma!" she
insisted heartily. "Everyone does." She had been a widow with four
small children with ages similar to his four. They married and had

four more together. Brit, or "D" as the kids all called him (short for Dad), worked long hours at the lab on his experiments. Lil acted as his administrator, typing his many grant proposals and managing the many visiting scientists, lab technicians, and students.

After a long day at work, Ma and D arrived home for dinner just before seven. We were served by the cook at the mahogany oval table in the dining room. A large roast of beef or pork came with almost every meal, along with potatoes, a vegetable, or salad. D carved thoughtfully, asking each of us questions about our day. He doled out small portions. We were careful not to talk unless spoken to. I had never seen so much food or eaten so little at the table.

Visiting scientists often were invited guests, occasionally a Nobel laureate. The dinner talk was almost exclusively about research, but occasionally about sailing. Lillie squirmed next to Maggie, who reached under the table and pinched with her sharp nails. At a signal, we jumped to clear the dishes. Lingering in the warmth of the kitchen and still hungry, we stuffed our mouths full of food. Later, gathering at the piano, we sang Billie Holiday, Lorenz Hart, and George Gershwin. Six-year-old Ben leaned against D while he played; our voices were thin and eager. Ma dozed on the couch; Sam was in bed; D went back to the lab for a few more hours of work.

I was absorbed into the Chance family. In the morning, before I took the train to school, I ate buttered toast, bacon, and jelly in the kitchen. In the evening I chased Ben, cornering him for a bath. I taught Lillie piano and sat with Maggie in her room. On fall weekends, we sailed on the Chesapeake Bay. In the winter we drove down to the New Jersey shore and shivered in the barely heated summer home in Mantoloking. I learned Morse code and sat in the laboratory, filling out reprint requests. And always I studied. None of my grades from Germany were transferred, and I was both determined and not sure I'd get into college.

By spring, tension filled the house. Icy silence grew between Ma and D, and she drank whisky in the evenings. She was often short with me. On weekends, Ma retreated to her farm in the suburbs and D went down to tend his sailboats in New Jersey. During the wedding of a daughter from Ma's first marriage, D abruptly left after the ceremony and took me sailing with a colleague. I was uncomfortable, baffled.

"Mrs. Chance always seems angry at me," I whispered to my mother on our weekly phone call.

"Don't be silly," my mother countered, "she is busy and overworked." She did not hesitate. "Make sure you help out."

Spring came to Philadelphia, saturated with flowers. My mother took another foreign exchange position, this time in Israel. I deferred my enrollment to Bennington College, planning to spend the year learning Hebrew, studying piano at the University of Tel Aviv, and dancing at the Bat-Dor Company School. I needed my passport renewed.

I chattered, worried, as D drove me down to the passport office. We were stuck in traffic on Walnut Street. The car windows were open, and a soft spring breeze scented with cherry blossoms filled the air.

My old passport with childhood photo and beautiful curling script listed me as Linda Christina Aney, my mother's maiden name. Since grade school I had been using my stepfather's name, Davidson, I explained to D, but it had never been legally changed.

The traffic inched forward, and we stopped again.

"Do you think," I wondered, "they would just add my Davidson name on?" The sun slanted in the car. I talked on, nervously going over what I was to say to convince the officials. D was silent.

What does a father do when he has been sworn to secrecy? His large, weathered hands held the steering wheel, the blunt nail of his thumb white with pressure, his curved lips pressed together. He stared ahead. He said nothing.

Chapter 14

LOVE

Philadelphia (1993)

It may help us, in those times of trouble, to remember that love is not only about relationship, it is also an affair of the soul. Disappointment in love, even betrayals and losses, serve the soul at the very moment they seem in life to be tragedies. The soul is partly in time and partly in eternity. We might remember the part that resides in eternity when we feel despair over the part that is in life.[1]

Thomas Moore

Shatter my heart so a new room can be created for a Limitless Love.[2]

Sufi Saying

January 17

Each holiday, my stepfather asks for a "Christmas amount" of information from me. I almost never hear from him during the year, but at Christmas he cheerfully calls out, "How are you doing, Tina?" He waits expectantly for a year's synopsis. Rage boils out of my stomach for the 364 days of disinterest. He towers over me. I pause.

Since I was five, I have dragged him behind me in an attempt to make him into the parent I need. His head over my shoulder,

I traveled through the years, stretching him until he became distorted. His feet are back when he married my mother, his body grotesquely elongated over these many years. "Let me go," he whispers hoarsely.

I want flesh and blood—human, passionate, and real. Instead I have a long, thin burden. I want a relationship; he wants gossip, his Christmas amount. And if I let him go? His face will slowly return to his feet; he will become a tiny figure, a small black silhouette. I am exhausted from this pulling.

We stand side by side on the soft blue carpet in my mother's living room. His absence and indifference crowd up against me. I look at him. Here, at this moment of time, this age, this portal, I see what I am doing. My need is in contrast to his incompetence. My desire stands in relief against his inability. In my mind's eye, I let him fall back, gracefully. A soft retreat to stand on the horizon.

To live beyond this reach is truly a miracle of life and the soul's desire to regenerate.

January 18

Work begins on a new piece for WHYY-TV called *Requiem for Something Lost (Back to the Room Beyond the Stairs, Those Terrible Secrets)*. They have commissioned several artists in different media to produce a three- to five-minute film. I will write the story, use the piece I wrote in 1986, and work with wonderful director Glenn Holsten to get the product I want.

Requiem for Something Lost describes a little girl going up a staircase. She is dressed in a white blouse and plaid skirt; her school shoes are scuffed and her laces half tied. She tugs at her hair as she slowly ascends the stairs. Hesitating, she backs down a step, sliding her hand down the banister. Is she being called or must she simply go? What is the terrible secret? She pauses. Welling up behind her is the music for three saxophones, their throaty voices pulsing and wailing.

She sits atop the stairs at the end of the film, leaning against the wall. Her skinny elbows rest on her knees; she waits. What else can little girls do? A faint hope, a prayer, a song.

My daughter will play the part of the little girl. At first I thought she was too old for the part, that little girls are sexually abused at a much earlier age. But several days into the filming I remember with a start, I was her age when I was abused. How had I forgotten this again?

The evening sky is dark blue when we emerge from the filming. Stars blink. The air is crisp and cold. Cassie runs to the car, laughing, her breath steaming out of her. I smile and feel the wonder of my life. None of it can hurt me or throw me into chaos now. I contain all; I disavow none.

January 19

I celebrate my fortieth birthday with a party. We drink champagne, eat decadent desserts, and keep the house full of dancing until late. I want my next forty years to be unexpected and planned, quiet and noisy, where I can be by myself or in the company of friends and loved ones, a life of sowing and reaping.

February 14

The Greater Twin City Youth Symphony gave a wonderful first performance of *The Selkie Boy* in Minneapolis. The orchestra consists of the best high school performers in the city; they were amazing in their abilities and energy. Young deaf students from the National Sign Company created a dramatization of the story for the performance. Signing and pantomiming, their young bodies took on the shape of the seals, their faces were bright and sparkling.

March 1

She steps close to me and almost whispers, "Can you have children and still have a career in music?" Attractive and young, she is a successful composer, already teaching at a prestigious university and married to an older, well-known composer. They are talking about having children, but she is not sure. I smile.

I can only speak for myself. Having my daughter opened me up in a way that I never could have imagined. Through her I found the courage to face my dark self, which has allowed me to speak truth in my music. She awoke in me the possibility of love given and love reciprocated, and connected me to lingering soft animal embraces and the wonder of discovering the world anew.

And yet, time is now not my own. As a mostly single parent, I craft careful structures for childcare, combinations of daycare and babysitters, which at any moment can fall through—an illness, an early dismissal, a snow day—all is in shatters and I am frantic. I sneak into my studio when she is occupied and feel the weight of my continual distraction.

Alix Kates Shulman, in her book, *Burning Questions*, says, "There is a passionate case to be made on either side, having your children or doing without, and both sides are for humanity. Have your babies or tie your tubes—whatever you decide, you'll find out soon enough that you've lost something precious."[3]

March 12

The "blizzard" of '93 descends, blanketing us in snow. The premiere of my saxophone concerto has been canceled. There is no chance of the performance being rescheduled. More discouragingly, I have not heard from Meet the Composer about the proposed residency with OperaDelaware, Newark Symphony, and the YWCA. Creating such a detailed proposal where I would work for three years in a community setting has opened up the dream of new work—in this case an opera, *Billy and Zelda*. Already I hear it in my ears.

March 13

I am irritable and jumpy. I lay the groundwork for the orchestra piece *They Come Dancing*. My last large piece, the saxophone concerto, initially disappointed me. In the end, however, it was balanced, relaxed, and open. The form and direction were confident.

Where do I want this new piece to go? In other words, where am I in my life? I feel the call to dive deep and think hard. I'm not sure what I lack.

For the first time in sixteen years, I am not in the security of a primary relationship. With my husband, I was able to put any anxiety aside and submerge into my cavern to swim the waters of the dark lagoon. Now, I must deal with "it" again: a future possible relationship. Sexuality, feelings of inadequacy, and loneliness sit with me now. Who will love me? Who will I allow to love me?

Is this what I must write about next—this sexuality, the desire to be coupled? Rhythms pound in my head. I dodge but am snagged. I remind myself to write more counterpoint. Why do I hear this call for unison? Jungle drums are loud, a primeval pounding. This heart of my life, heat, and love.

March 15
Feeling close to the earth.

March 22
After weeks of being a single parent, Cassie is finally at her father's for the weekend. I sleep late, make tea, and think about starting to date again. It has been over a year since Wood and I separated.

March 25
During my massage, I wept. My first instinct was to laugh, but my face was a grimace. Looking at me, she said softly, "It's sometimes hard to take." The smell of sage and the kneading of my feet broke something deep inside of me. She wiped my face like a baby. The hot cloth soothed me.

I am crying for a piece. I feel the sound of wood, a depth of rhythm.

March 26
This day of March is warm and sunny. The melting snow makes rivers out of pathways. I sit under a tree with a pile of pine cone sheaves—a squirrel's compost heap. She chatters overhead while dropping bits of trash. "I am here," I whisper. She warns me not to come near.

Tomorrow, there will be snow again, six inches is predicted. I feel gloriously and gratefully alive. The early morning yoga class and food at the Kripalu Center, deliciously filled with strange spices and yogurt sauces. Soon a new piece.

March 31

"What is the relationship between artists and their work?" a friend asks.

I can only speak of my landscape—to economize my life so that I am available. Not as an act of abstinence or poverty, instead an act of allowing. When my life is work-centered, all else falls off. I am at the essence of my life. The choice is time, energy, and clarity. The rest—family, friends, fun—falls into place naturally.

Being available is an act of love I give myself, for here is where my spirit lives. As I go out in my work, it is all me, and at the same time, not me. When my work connects with others, my face becomes many faces, both anonymous and personal, both unrecognizable and identifiable.

The risk of art is to be at the edge of selfness, which seems to be vanity, but is not. Vanity keeps me separate and elevated from others. Art grovels in the same mud, but ascends.

For today, I ask what my work needs and thereby know how to live my life. Letting the non-essentials go, I keep the treasures. The rest flows from me like fall leaves tossed on the river stream, riding the current happily away from me. The love I put into my work is the same that pours into my life, family, and community. A source that renews itself continually.

April 1

I am overwhelmed by my sexuality this past month. I am full of fantasies; I scarcely know what to do. Need to exhale. Need to dance.

April 6

I am in between a state of reluctance and anticipation. I can "hear" the new work better than I can understand it—something about mountains, fires, sexuality, and the dark pounding of the heart.

April 7

Spring is finally here. The magnolia's dark pink buds are ready to burst with color and joy. Quiet and peaceful, I yearn to open to this new piece like these buds.

I sense the work, the crackling of the opening. I suddenly remember a dream I had several years ago. Standing in an open field, I am behind a camera ready to photograph a large white horse lying on a flowered couch. I cannot get the entire horse in my view finder; I am too close. I step back, and the clouds part. I look up and see the red glow of the peaks—fire on the mountain.

The dream filled me with love, sexuality up on the mountain, glowing and hot. This is where I need to go, into the heat of the fire, which is myself.

I hear the beginning, muted piano. The marimba and vibraphone use fingers on the instrument bars instead of mallets. The rhythms widen and deepen, a counterpoint. But always a linear pull.

April 13

I am exhausted from hours in the studio, recording my piece *Bleached Thread, Sister Thread* with the Mendelssohn Quartet for the CRI label. I don't dare listen to the hundreds of takes for a while. My ears are numb.

In the evening, I go to a friend's for dinner. They invite a colleague of theirs from work. He is handsome. I sit next to him at the table, our thighs almost touching. Before I leave, he asks me out.

April 14
The form my music takes is a stream of movement, a consciousness liquid enough to become something else at any moment. Lean and snake-like, the form is continually circular and linear, transforming in a seamless continuity. I know it is good; I also doubt it.

April 16
Composer Morton Feldman reportedly said, "Most composers are limited by one form." Finding a level of comfort, they stay with it. I wonder about mine and if I should relook at it. Press on, explore it further.

Forms or approaches are inherently archetypal. Like jewels hidden deep in the earth, not all have been found. The work of an artist is to reveal the ones overlooked and connect us, the present us, with their magic in new ways.

April 18
I go to a wonderful performance by composer and performer Laurie Anderson. In her program notes she wrote, "The mind is like a wild white horse, and when you build a corral for it, be careful that it is not too small. And when your house is burning, walk away."[4]

April 19
My piece *Fire on the Mountain* smolders with the fire within me. I bring the fire of my life home—the urge to renew myself, to integrate and combine with others. Sacred and profane, intangible and tangible come together in wonder and beauty. It spills off me, like seeds on a rich earth. Ripe and overflowing, succulent and juicy, the surrender is to the sweet body. The delicious needs and urges.

April 22
So, it is true. When it comes to love, I have the same bad gene as my Chance father. No restraint at all. I have fallen into love, into bed, into flesh.

May 4
Today I am grounded. I explore the difference between the horizontal (up and down) and the circular. Fire—love, intimacy, and passion—are continuous and scattered. Flames erupt suddenly, becoming large, then extinguish. Growth is both linear and not.

May 5
The moon crests this week. Quickly undone by this romance, my nights are terrible and I wake continually at 4:00 a.m. Daydreams keep me up late and exhaust me during the day. I work to bring myself back to earth, but the fantasies are like an addiction—they possess me.

Integration and being present are unending difficulties. With this tumultuous time, stability is essential. Patience, patience! The real direction of this new romance will be revealed.

May 6

After a day of being sucked down the emotional rapids, he called and I am on the shore again, basking lazily in the sun. Today I am smooth and continuous, half-drugged.

Now, to work on my piece *Fire on the Mountain*. The Monday morning itch to sit in my cool studio with bare feet to write is strong.

July 21

It is an uneven time again; he is taking a break from our relationship. Yesterday I sat with a fellow artist for a long time. She looked off for a moment, then said, "You'll get through it. Don't panic. You have to pay for what you get." She smiled, touched my arm. "Don't fight it so much; it's part of the package. There is an end to it. It will come clear. What is the alternative? Bear it long enough and you will be fine."

The evening is cool, and I listen to the hum of the cicadas, the murmuring of the traffic. The dog's collar clinks, and Cassie's footstep creaks on the floorboards. The weight of my childhood presses me hard, awoken by this affair. Nothing, I think, was this difficult; nothing will be this arduous.

As my life becomes clear and resonant, the ragged truth is revealed; once I am able to feel joy, vulnerability and fear are not far behind. Even amid the blackness of yesterday, I felt the cool blue wind of the day on the hairs of my forearm and smiled.

July 22

I finished *Fire on the Mountain* today. It was difficult to write, full of the energy of love, storm, and pain, and finally the bursting of the heart to a quiet, open melody.

I am reminded again of my dream of the horse and the mountain. Often, I stand too close to love and intimacy. All I can see is the whiteness of love's flanks and abdomen, but not the fine outline of the body, the suppleness of the neck, and the quietly etched flair of the nostrils.

So I step back. What is the alternative?

July 26

"Pain is the touch of the great mother teaching us to bear and grow in rapture. She has three stages of her schooling, endurance, next is equanimity of soul, last ecstasy."[5]

Equanimity—evenness of temper, calmness. Ecstasy—rapture, transport.

August 1

I sit out in this creeping dark August heat to write and read. Cassie comes down to razz me, wrapped in bed sheets. Her long hair tosses, her black eyes snap, and her lips pout. I hold fast. She kisses the dog and goes stamping to bed, determined to snarl her way to sleep, like all good eight-year-olds. The sprinkler throws water up in the air; the evening, this moment, is lovely. And yet, as I press outward toward the next day, or the next week, I feel the difficulties of decisions, the sadness of passing time. I try not to wonder what is to come.

There is inconsistency between the moment and the future. My music is both the present and the unrecognized future, contained in one. To dream of a better life is to push beyond all that is known into a future of possibilities. What is the balance between them all? Shall I always be learning from the past, living the moment, and imaging the future as movement into the light?

And how do I bear the loss of this relationship? When will it be clear?

August 5

Cool breezes pick up the hair around my face. We sail in the Barnegat Bay, then anchor and eat cookies. D, my Chance father, leans against the bulkhead of the boat, and we talk of work. He makes for great company.

Fantasy is inauthentic control. When I am in an authentic place, I act and deal with the present. When I wish or fantasize, I try to control the future by making it up. Inauthentic living.

Work is always a haven.

The past month I have been out of control; I lost my balance in the midst of love. The good news is that when I fall out of the boat, I can get back in. The nature of healing comes with time and experience.

August 26

Cassie and I are down at the shore for a week. I start to think clearly about my next orchestra piece, *They Come Dancing*. I reread the full version of *Black Elk Speaks*.

> Then the bay horse spoke to me again and said: "See how your horses all come dancing!" I looked, and there were horses, horses everywhere—a whole skyful of horses dancing round me.

They are dancing.
They are coming to behold you.
The horse nation of the west is dancing.
They are coming to behold![6]

My palms chafe. The music comes through my upturned hands. My palms are ready and turned toward the light. Being with Eva and her family at the shore is a healing grace. I hear them in the kitchen, the dishes clinking, puffs of laughter; I am soothed. Next week a blue moon.

August 28
What is the vision of this new piece? The gathering and coming together of community, a circle is formed, turning darkness into light. Pounding becomes linear beauty, a driving force, heat of our loins, and passion of our lives. My piece is about the transformation of the dark side of power, the pounding downward to light, to the vibrations of colors and life.

August 29
They Come Dancing runs across the plains, wide-open spaces with joyous freedom. The gathering is the movements of life, circular and horizontal, joyous through the grass, across the plains. They come dancing, stomping, and jumping with intricate hand movements. They come pounding, the dark heat and passion reveal the dark side of renewal and destruction. Light transforms into ribbons of color, the vibrations of love. Renewal comes in beating chords, shimmering, vibrating.

The vision is the joyful leaping and dancing of being alive, a state that lets us taste the body and soul. Dark and deep, this is the fulcrum of transcendence—through the heat we become other, the spiritual, the vibration. That which is above and beyond our lives and bodies.

September 1
Today I lie under purple flowered sheets in the coolness of the morning and watch the gray clouds. The ocean roars, and I walk barefoot along the wet surf. The doors and windows are open and unlocked. September lawns are still green. I read and nap all day. Lulled by the sea, I am near the constancy of my family. The weekend is full of laughter and good food—of not having to think or be alone.

September 3
What foolishness did I open myself up to again? I had intended to stay away from him, keep myself safe. I blush at my carelessness.

September 8
The day is dark and rainy. "Aver from memory," I write with bright pink lipstick on my bathroom mirror in great cursive script.

How do I keep myself from being my own nature? Wouldn't it be best if I dig him out of my body like a deer tick, take my medicine and move on?

September 11
Beautiful cool morning—a good Philadelphia autumn day—blue sky and high sunlit trees. The wind outside picks up once in a while, blowing flowers over. There is so much I do not understand. Love is one. Its realm mysterious and dark.

My music dreams of the flow and the brilliance of love between two people. The gathering, the smile between two strangers, oneness.

September 13

I wake early, flooded with dreams at night, colorful and disconnected. Saturated by the morning, I hardly remember anything. The rest of the day seems unbearable. Grief oozes out of me. I ache all over.

Yet, the day is also beautiful. I start my orchestra piece and receive news of another commission. I lunch with a wonderful and beautiful dear friend. Cassie has her first full day of school.

September 15

In the evenings, I take a watercolor class at Fleisher Art Memorial. At first, I am disconnected and quiet. But color catches my attention. The model's flesh is warm and full of shades. I experiment with colors I previously disdained and am overcome with the sensuousness of shapes. My brush is my hand. I paint her shoulders and neck as if I were touching them.

The length and intensity in the orchestra piece is of critical importance. The rhythmic pounding needs to continue until it is almost unbearable. Life's energy comes out of the dry grasses and sparks the dance of life with joy, destruction, and renewal. They catch fire—the quickening of life, the consumption and rebirth. The music is a movement from dry pulsing rhythms to pure sound and harmony.

The opening section is written. In pairs, trios, and solos, they run across the plains. Stopping to dance briefly, they dash on. It is infectious, contagious. Joy of the body, and the shimmering other.

September 17

I am up early. The morning is still dark with cheeping crickets. Their hum is constant and optimistic. A lightness and quickness are coming back to me, a sense of connectedness.

But last night I dreamed I found an old letter of parchment folded up into a square. I open it carefully to find half a rusting nail, a bullet. The piece was cut longwise and the rust was smeared on the paper. Then I remembered a deep wound, up through my body, through my abdomen and uterus. I search my memory. Was I prostrate when the bullet shot through me?

September 26

I am up in Oneonta over the weekend to work with Lâle and Eva on the opera, *Billy and Zelda*. I contracted the cold-flu everyone has down here, so I spent a day lying down in Eva's house, happily being with others while I was seeped in illness. We completed much of the libretto.

Or could I be pregnant? I am overdue. The last time we slept together I was careless, pretending we were not breaking up. My body has a ripe feel to it, with heavy breasts, rounded abdomen, and translucent skin.

September 28

Yesterday, it rained and flooded. A tornado touched down. By evening, a beautiful double rainbow lit the sky. Today is cool, clear, and sunny. So will it be with my life. I move ahead with clarity. I trust that what comes next will be full of all of life's pleasure, pain, and connectedness.

The fall beckons me forward. The air is sharp and clear. Deep love exacts no payment and takes no prisoners; it is characterized by generosity and continuity. It harbors no grudges. Neither is it witless, but vast and knowing.

September 30
Over the summer, I lost contact with the greater whole and forfeited my connectedness with others. I blush. Love disconnects to connect, and through that, deepens the bond to all of life. When I lost love, I lost my connection to myself. I was not to be found.

October 11
Adele sits with me and holds my hand. The procedure is over and I am in bed resting. She brings me a cup of tea. She is quiet, patient.

The distance between my body, my heart, and my mind in terms of understanding is vast. I have felt this pregnancy and abortion through my body, but my mind lags far behind, perplexed. I feel humility to my body experience and a supplication beyond words. I am exhausted by loss.

October 14
Philadelphia is full of noise. The cars passing late at night, the swoosh of the trolley, the rattle of empty trucks, screeching brakes. But here, in Mt. Gretna, all is peaceful. Occasionally the wind picks up the tree branches, then stillness again. I need to press on now, both closer to my work and out into the future. Ever this diving deep and surfacing. The work at hand is vital.

In love's embrace, I lost my desire to compose and replaced it with the desire to feel. Never have I lived so in my body. It was a kind of frenzy, accompanied by a sense of urgency and lifetime deprivation. Touch, taste, smell were alive, full, and tremendously large, each meal succulent, every touch exquisite. Now, like wishing for one's lost youth, I want it back. I have only just awakened. Who would not fight to hold on to that sensuality and body gratification? It is beyond pleasure; it is the body finally sighing in release, "This is how it ought to be."

The head, the heart, and the body.

I turn toward my orchestra piece. How do I fit my experience into the work? I feel out this piece in the dark, snuffling and sniffing, knowing the danger of pressing too hard. I need the work, to fall deep into it. Without it, I lose my balance, but paradoxically, without life's fullness, passion, and disappointment, I have nothing to write about. Always this terrible balance.

October 15

I have a deep sense of not knowing anything, only feeling with my body and heart. I simply do not understand. I can only move on slowly, achingly. Music is home, where I go for quiet, connection, and comfort. I rest there, not knowing. Then I press on, pour myself into. I live peaceably until it is time.

October 25

My work is intense these days, and I slip into my music world. I walk on errands or go to meetings. The sound of my piece pulls at me; another world that I tune into. It is a house full of children learning how to romp. I peer in through the windows to see how things are progressing. I am present and often sit quietly with my mind elsewhere.

November 2

The day is wild; dark clouds and winds whip the house, storming and fussing. I lie in bed in the afternoon thinking of my piece, watching the clouds being tossed. The wind rages and moans.

What is this soul-missing? I don't know how to turn it around, and can only seem to live through it. I want the balance of things, the togetherness and the separateness. I wait for my soul to bloom, to burst into song, into a riot of color. I can dance by myself, but want to dance with another. I can sing a solo, but wish to tune to a duet. And I crave this the way one craves nourishment of food and water. I do not want caviar, but the colorful dark greens and reds of life.

How do I place my longing in context and address it with trust? I cannot deny this soul hunger, because it is also a soul search. I often squander my present for the future. I need to trust and not fight it so much. Living is to accept all of life as it is now.

To be heard and to be found. I have to smile. Years ago I came across the quote by philosopher Lewis Mumford; at the heart of artistic endeavor "is to be heard but not to be found." In the early years of my composing, I wanted nothing more than this—to tell my story and not be revealed. In the next span of time I wanted just to be heard and seen.

Now I simply want the latter—to be found, named, and called.

November 6

I am getting at something. There are two parts of me, the solid self and the optimist. My solid self knows and connects. She does not mince words, is practical, determined, and sure-footed. She knew the first time I kissed him that there was no possibility for a permanent relationship and sensed the difficulties that lay ahead.

The optimist is positive, encouraging, and girlish. She attempts to raise my hopes by excusing behavior. "He really doesn't mean it," she comforts. "Talk to him, he'll understand!" She frowns while concentrating. When she presses or manages, her hands flutter. Her emotions are held in balance by outside circumstances and buffeted about on the winds of the others' lives. Breathless, she is wildly happy one moment; the next, all hopes are dashed. "Love will never happen," she cries anxiously.

My solid self laughs, "Of course it will!"

I am always surprised by how much power the optimist has in my life. She is wily and works behind the scenes. I am caught short. Who is this stranger manipulating, pleading, and wheedling behind my back? Why do I recognize her so clearly?

The optimist takes over when I am vulnerable. When the relationship starts to splutter, she panics. Revved into high gear, she is off and running, trying to fix things. When she fails, she sinks into chaos. The solid self works hard. She plods quietly along, gaining back ground that the optimist spent. At times she just is; she knows.

The optimist writes pleading letters. The solid self refuses to send them. The optimist delights in fantasy. The solid self refuses to dwell. The solid self gets her hair done. The optimist waits and looks sad. The solid self goes out on dates. The optimist is crushed when he is not the one she is looking for.

But I like the optimist, her fire and spirit. She enters like a fireman, trumpets blazing. "Don't worry! I'm here!" she cries, spraying her hose wildly, damaging furniture. She is crazy and full of life. Then she is squinty-eyed and scared. The solid self says little. She is calm, centered, and unflappable. At times, she is quiet and hidden. The optimist darts around so much, one can hardly tell what's happening. I do not want to be rid of her. But she does a lot of damage.

Who is it, then, that feels life is empty without a relationship? Who feels this soul-missing, a deep missing? The solid self lifts up her face and sniffs at the wind. The optimist shakes her head; she doesn't know. Another, further back—oh, little one on Solvig's knee?

November 7
The optimist is crushed. She feels found and unloved; she sits deflated, waiting to be expelled.

November 16
The weather is unbelievably warm. A gentle look on my daughter's face, we run outdoors in our undershirts.

November 19
A total eclipse of the full moon. I stay up late to watch the growing thumbprint over the face of the moon.

The reading at the bar mitzvah service is the story of Jacob, who wrestles all night with the angel. At daybreak, the angel is exhausted. "You must let me go."

Still, Jacob holds on. "Bless me first," he demands.

I listen, transfixed. My angel is of loneliness and abandonment. How do I ask for a blessing and let go? After the eclipse, I lie in bed under the cool light that fills my room.

December 2

What is a blessing? It can be a gift bestowed of friendship or healing. It can be good health, family, life, and work. A blessing is also an open palm pressed against a forehead—a father's blessings. The dictionary definition is "to consecrate by religious rite, make or pronounce holy, to bestow good of any kind upon, to protect or guard from evil, to request of God the bestowal of divine favor, to extol as holy, glorify."

If I received a blessing each day, what would it be? I am embarrassed and feel histrionic, foolish. What do I hold on to? Where are my bearings? I try to reckon with the nature of imperfection.

Today's blessing is fragility. With the ease of breaking comes the ability to feel; in the possibility of rupture lies deep love. Fragility is the companion to strength. Like a contrast color or foil, one needs the other. Otherwise, strength is unskilled and rigid.

Fragility is strength's humility. It is silent and respectful of the ability to shatter and break, to splinter into a thousand pieces. Fragility teaches me human limits and tender vulnerability.

Perhaps the first blessing is love—that I loved deeply, whether the outcome is good or bad. The second blessing is fragility, the ability to break at the deepest feelings.

December 7

My life is on a hinge; it turns slowly. I have a Rip Van Winkle dream, a "time to get up" dream. Abundance. Time to clean up.

December 31

Today is a snowy, slushy day. All is quiet. Cassie and her friend play together while I lie in bed with my tea and journal. I call out for them to stop teasing the dog, who whines for a walk. I feel the power and energy of my life, the deep connection, the work, the joy, and the sorrow. It is all about the capacity to feel, which by its very nature is a mixed blessing.

I think again about Jacob wrestling with his angel. In his struggle, he experiences how great the divine is.

How great the divine.

Chapter 15

THE OCEAN

The beach house in Mantoloking is Chance domain, spacious and ramshackle. Rooms fold into rooms, sand crunches underfoot, and towels litter the back porch by the outside shower. The large dining table seats twenty. The kitchen sink is piled with cereal bowls and glasses of half-finished milk. Bedroom doors are ajar; windows are thrown open. Sparsely furnished, the house is a way station to clear, blue summer days.

The spiral staircase curls up to my father's room. On the third floor, the aerie views both the bay and the ocean. D's straight key for sending Morse code messages and his ham radios are stacked on the desk. The static is constant, broken only by an occasional garble. He looks through the binoculars at the sleek and elegant E Scow sailboat fleet on the bay. They edge up to the starting line, each trying to find its position. He puts his hand on my shoulder.

The house was always full on summer weekends. A two-hour drive from Philadelphia over the Walt Whitman Bridge, we skirted weekend traffic through back roads toward the Pine Barrens, acres of rare pygmy pitch pines. Stopping only to buy ripe New Jersey tomatoes and corn, we were finally at the Mantoloking drawbridge, waiting for a sailboat to languidly pass under the upturned bridge.

Friday's dinner was the traditional picnic at the yacht club. My father and I walked over as the sun set over the bay, flooding us with red light. Soon, however, he disappeared into a group of friends, and I stood awkwardly with a plate of food balanced in my hand.

"So, where do you fit in?" A man smiled pleasantly at me. He is a friend of the family. "We know the Chances well, and I don't remember if you are from the first or the second marriage." His voice trailed off. His wife leaned toward me, anticipating my reply.

My voice was more shrill than I expected. "Who knows! We haven't figured it out yet," I dodged.

Although I'm not a secret in the Chance world, I do not broadcast that I was born between families—on the wrong side of the blanket, a *nullius filius*, more commonly known as illegitimate.

D caught my hand as we walked back to the house. Lillie and Maggie have run to put on their bathing suits for an evening swim.

"They think you're my girlfriend," he said conspiratorially. "Let them think!" He laughed delightedly.

Later, I lay in the front bedroom of the house and listened to the halyards clink on the masts of the sailboats docked on the bay. On the Chance side, our relatedness is measured by the crookedness of our bottom teeth: Elle, Britty, Jan, Peter, Maggie, Lillie, Ben,

Sam, Jan M., Neil, and me. There may be others, we suspect. When D finally got a vasectomy at seventy, we all sighed in collective relief.

The breeze is tinged with coolness. Eva, Scott, Lâle, and Loren. Kjell-Olof, Sven-Johan, Sölve and Ulf.

I can almost hear the ocean.

Chapter 16

RETURN

Philadelphia (1994)

The mind creates the abyss; the heart crosses it.
Sri Nisargadatta Maharaj

Grief is a sword, or it is nothing.
Paul Monette

January 27

These are good working days. The orchestra piece comes out easily, and I feel a rush of anticipation. The work whispers around me all day like angel wings, brushing my cheeks, fluttering and dancing.

I bathe in performances of my music. Last week, *I Hear the Mermaids Singing* was warmly received at Carnegie Hall. The performance was sensuous and beautiful. Now for a few days in Lexington, Virginia, as a composer-in-residence.

February 11

The snow continues. Another day of being trapped inside. Another day of not being able to move forward. I dreamed gray twilight crept toward me like mist. Circling arms around me, it grew into arms of longing.

February 25

Snowfall again, beautiful and heavy. A dark, sleepy day. I return to bed in the morning and sleep a deep dreamless sleep. I am growing something for the next part of my piece.

Composing *They Come Dancing* is never in a straight line. Work has gone well up to the fast section, the dark rumbling before the timpani race. Then it took two days just to unwind a small section, the harmonies were tangled up in the moving lines. The work insists on the extra time and consideration, even when I don't want to give it.

Theophany: the appearance of God.

March 8

The premiere of *Fire on the Mountain* at the Ethical Society went very well. The work is rugged and open. I try not to delight in the *Philadelphia Inquirer* review, but can't help myself.

"The piece is rhythmically driving, with fascinatingly simple yet lovely harmonic changes. The composer makes music satisfying by carefully managing tension and release; it's being able to bring a sense of beauty and emotion to a strict organizational structure, a rarity in any age."

March 9

In the evenings I read Greek myths to Cassie. So many are stories of love. Bellerophon tames Pegasus with the magic bridle, but releases him in pity. Now free, the winged horse shoots up into the air, out of sight, then comes back. Having tasted companionship, he returns for love. Atalanta spurns her suitors, but finally agrees to marry the man who can beat her in a foot race. As she runs against Hippomenes, he tosses three golden apples, one at a time. The apples, filled with his love, sidetrack her. She stops to retrieve them, losing the race.

Love distracts, love attracts. Love brings the solitary into companionship, to give and receive love.

March 17

The orchestra piece is almost complete. I have been composing steadily for seven months. There are still some revisions to do, expansions and changes to the orchestration, but all in all, the work is good. I have gained depth in my work. It is dark in a rooted way, more intimate and sensual than before.

March 16

I am a sorry line dancer. Bumping into fellow dancers, I step on countless toes and kick my legs when I should be lifting my arms. Neither, however, am I an outlaw. Constantly out of place and blaming the system, an outlaw is a wearying and self-destructive proposition. Love continues to be the path I choose.

March 21

The first day of spring. I rake leaves with a vengeance, uncovering the crocus shoots and closed flower buds. The sky is blue-blue and the sun warm. The orchestra piece is finished. I will miss being in its center.

They Come Dancing brings men and women together. The men are strong and handsome, their skin wet with sweat. The women are full-hipped and stunning. Beating the earth with their bare feet, they are all beautiful to me.

April 5

I just received confirmation that the three-year Meet the Composer residency is funded. Delight and deep tiredness sweep over me. Knowing I am both finished with the orchestra piece and that we will be financially in good shape for the next few years releases me. I sleep, read, and sleep some more. I could sleep for weeks.

I am planning a six-week trip to Sweden, a sabbatical from composing. I need to lie fallow for a while.

May 8

Days follow one after another. Some are quiet and full of work, and others tumble around, see-sawing. I fluctuate from calm to hyper-anxious. On good days, I am open to the understanding of the world. On bad days, I feel the full fury of my emotions running half out of control. They are like wild horses, beautiful and strong. Once frightened, however, they panic and thrust their huge weight around.

May 12

A dark, glowering day threatens rain at any minute. My garden reeks of flowers—opulence gone mad. Blossoms hang in every direction, blues and purples against pink, buds swollen with possibility. My life is calm and rooted, full of colors and movements. No task seems mundane or out of place. Distress holds possibility. I have gone through the euphoria of my fortieth year, been tossed around by love, and emerged on my feet and working hard. I am awake and alert, conscious of my strength, and not afraid of who I am.

The skies suddenly break into a downpour, a steady drumming of water. The darkness of the clouds drains out to make way for the light.

June 1
I throw myself into my work. I abandon myself to it. Before me lies my orchestra piece to copy, the Meet the Composer residency plan to complete, and the trip to Sweden to plan.

Yesterday, I went to a luncheon of one of the residency partners, the YWCA. I am humbled by the women with whom I will be working. They make a difference in the lives of the underprivileged and work with dedication to change the face of America. Truly subversive acts.

June 5
Early, the birds scold and cluck. I sit on the back porch, my tea steaming. My work waits for me. The morning is mine.

June 6
It is the anniversary of D-day. My mind has been with my neighbor Chris and her son Billy. My new opera for OperaDelaware is based, in part, on her story of Billy.

I was in my last week of pregnancy with Cassie when I visited Chris. Her apartment was dark, and clocks ticked as we talked about children over tea. It was almost time to go; I impulsively asked her about her son, Billy. Perhaps it was the growing darkness or my advanced state of pregnancy, but she began to tell me a story she rarely told anyone.

She was a young and recently divorced woman. Moving from the West, she soon established herself as one of the first female realtors in Philadelphia in the '30s. Billy was her beloved son who planted roses with her in the front yard. Suddenly the war started, and he secretly enlisted without her consent. He was nineteen when he died on the shores of Normandy.

"My sisters had so many sons, so many sons who went to war, in submarines," she ruefully said. "They all came back."

She did not believe Billy was dead and refused to allow the military to bring him back from France. "It was not his body," she maintained. For decades, she was certain he was somewhere, shell-shocked. She pointed to a box next to her chair—all his letters that she still could not, these many decades later, bear to read again.

We sat quietly. The sun had now set; she rose to turn on the lights. Billy was there with us, an uneasy ghost. What is this relationship with our children that continues even when they are dead?

June 10

I want to rethink the restless and driving quality in my works. I listened to Bach's Brandenburg Concertos. His energy is such a pleasure, never tense or irritable. I am letting his music brew in my thoughts.

June 21

I have lunch with my friend Ayella. Her face peeks out of her wild, curly hair with a sweet smile and flashing white teeth. We talk about choice and living in the present. There is a kind of hopelessness to trying to decide on the basis of right or wrong, white or black, yes or no.

"You need," Ayella says in her thick Israeli accent, "to use another part of your knowing." She pauses a moment. "Ask not what is right or wrong; instead, what is the next task."

June 22
We are down for the weekend at the shore with Eva. We walk on the beach in the evening; the moon is half hidden in the clouds, a misty luminescence. The sea, both cold and hot, throws off the smell of the underwater world, then disappears in a thunder of waves. Sophie dances before me on the end of her leash. She stops to sip the salty water, throws up her head, and prances on air. It has been long since I sank my heels deep in the sand.

June 30
Time slows before we leave for Sweden. I shed responsibilities and emerge out of an overworked, tense, and irritable swirling mass. Amid the packing and getting ready, there is a tinge of sadness and loneliness. Leaving is difficult for me and has the scent of the past; my mother leaving me at eight months, my leaving Solvig, leaving my beloved Istanbul, and now leaving for Sweden.

I have been lonely since before my birth. My mother tells me she wept every day of her pregnancy with me.

July 1
"Reality, based on an understanding of the totality and oneness of existence, is as an unbroken and seamless whole."

"The mind may have a structure similar to the universe and in the underlying movement we call empty space there is actually a tremendous energy, a movement," claims David Bohm.

July 2

It begins. A trip into the past, present, and future. What do I want? Open space to think. Time to be with the sadness of my birth. Time to let it go.

To be free to go. To return with a softer-looking face.

July 5

"Why is the measure of love loss?" asks Jeanette Winterson in her moving novel *Written on the Body*. "Love demands expression."[1]

July 7

Our trip, so far, has been excellent. We had a seven-hour layover in London before flying on. Cassie and I napped on our bags. We stayed in Copenhagen, ate dinner, and went on a long walk. The weather is bright and clear.

My foster brother picked us up in Ålvesta, about an hour away from Gislaved in southern Sweden. It was good to see him again.

Tall and thin, Kjell-Olof speaks in an undertone. Often I can't understand him. I nod until I am forced to ask him to repeat himself. Recently married, he and his wife, Inger, live in a yellow clapboard house on a hundred-acre farm. The original homestead is a small, low-ceiling wooden house that's over two hundred years old.

Inger is slender, with a lovely face and a square chin. Her black-frame glasses make her face look hard and fragile at the same time. Her teenage children, Sabine and Joachim, are always laughing and talk to us in excellent English.

They have rented us a cottage, a *stuga*, two miles from their house. Without running water and electricity, the tiny house sits on the edge of a pine forest by one of Sweden's many lakes.

Blueberry bushes are on one side of the house, rocks and mosses on the other. I sit at the kitchen table writing by candlelight, overlooking the lake. The late evening sky is filled with pinks of sunset, glowing against the water. Still and quiet, it is a country where there is almost no dark during the summer months, only this cool air in twilight.

July 8

We sleep late, waking at nine to eat breakfast outside and paint a watercolor of the lake. I am at a still point in my life, a place of neither moving forward nor going back, just present, quiet, and still. Receptive. I have such an urge to write in my journal or write letters, as if I could pour myself out onto pages like liquid.

July 10

Kjell-Olof spends long hours with me. He laughs. I don't pronounce my name right, he says—it's Tina with your tongue caught behind your teeth almost as if you are lisping—"Thina!" Softer and longer. The morning is cool. We have milk with fresh strawberries and blueberries.

Stories are told that I have never heard. He tells me family myths where I am the subject. The day we decided to play Christmas and quietly flung pillow feathers all over the room for snow. When I peeled all the wallpaper off behind my bed, to just below the bed line. Potty trained together, we raced down the hallway, our bottoms glued on the porcelain bowls, our feet like racer cars.

Have I always missed him, my playmate, my twin?

July 12

The day is filled with people, talk, and things to see and do. I become overloaded. I long for quiet and dream of a new piece.

When people fill my space, I lose the ability to breathe. Tense and irritable, my internal private energy bottles up, my joints ache, my forearms grow hot and itchy. I move about restlessly. I need solitude to be healthy, and yet, I am haunted by a crushing sense of loneliness—the longing to be in the heat of my mother's breath and in the eyes of the beloved.

As a small child, I lost more than Solvig—I lost myself. As a child, I did not have an identity outside of my foster parents. I looked into the face and eyes of love and saw myself as loveable. As she supported me, I reached out and took a few steps to independence before falling back into her arms.

In my abrupt, silent departure from Sweden, I lost the thread of that life story. Solvig died to me, and with her, my continuity and assurance. I comforted myself with childish narcissism; it must be my fault. The mirror of reflected love was shattered. I replaced it with darkness, blame, and loneliness.

Solvig was my source. I search to be reunited to her. In an ordinary experience, we grow up and learn that our parents are in us. We no longer need them to know love. But having suffered this loss, I search for the ability to see myself.

Journey's end may be in sight not because I have found Solvig but because I have found myself. It is always the same thing.

I have grown up. I have become the full fruit of a mother's labor. What I lost—the love, the care, the creative, the intelligent—I now am. Solvig's love is complete. What I seek, I already have. What I long for, I am.

July 14

Andres, the little boy from the nearby farmhouse, visits us often. He speaks no English. He and Cassie push each other around. I hear them laughing and making exaggerated claims of being hurt. The sun slides off their brown backs, their hips are slim, their faces upturned. They are beautiful.

Odd, isn't it, this telling and retelling to remember? My tongue runs over the smooth stones of memory. I tell of myself, recreating it anew each time, seeing from different angles. I open myself up like a window on a crisp morning.

The flies fly in and out of our *stuga*. The outside cools off the insides. How lovely the evening, how crisp the night air. The last pinks and blues are above the mountain and glow on the water. The trees are darkly silhouetted. The birds call to each other in the dusk of midsummer. The warmth of the candles, the scratch of my pen.

July 17

I read *Eros the Bittersweet* by Anne Carson. A pithy, scholarly treatise on love, that "love is a suspended moment of living hope."[2]

"The desire to bring the absent into presence, or to collapse far from near, is also a desire to foreclose then upon now." [3]

I think of Solvig. "The moment Eros enters you," Carson says, "You perceive what you are, what you lack, what you could be. 'Now' is the gift of the gods, and an access into reality."[4]

July 18

We picked strawberries today. Bending over the plants in the hot sun, we found hordes of hidden fruit. The rich dark reds peeked out of the leaves, wet and juicy. The juice ran down my hands as I picked and ate, the fruit almost too ripe. The day was bright with clouds, both hot and cool.

July 19

I love to hear the Swedes talk. The language is both melodious and guttural. Almost lisping, they place the accent heavily on the first syllable in a precise kind of way. They follow a conversation closely with grunts and noises of assent or appreciation, inhaling heavily to show confirmation. The *ja* (yes) is swallowed.

The countryside and towns are beautifully kept. Gardens are luxurious yet simple, the landscape has a European neatness and beauty, with little that is outlandish or garish. Swedes are unaffected by the need to be individualistic in the way Americans are, so there is a uniformity to the beauty and a cleanliness that allows the eye and the soul to relax.

July 20

The Swedish woods stretch endless into darkness. The mosses are deep, and the greens are almost unbearable in their intensity and softness. The pines stand military straight, their lower limbs hang like skeleton arms. The trunks of the trees are covered with lichen and fungus, giving the bark a whitish look. The woods beckon and are foreboding, enticing me in an eerie sort of way. I understand the stories of elves and trolls and have glimpsed some of the impish spirits myself in the dark shadows.

But it is time for bed. The moon rises behind the firs. Even now the days grow shorter, the evening forecasts the coldness of autumn.

July 21

We are aboard the Silja Lines traveling to Turku from Stockholm. The ocean liner is enormous, full of duty-free stores and gambling. Cassie is in love with slot machines. At first she made much more than she started with, then lost it all. She frowns with bad temper.

I sit onboard the deck and watch a beautiful man. His face is lean, his hair gray. He sits, shifts, folds and unfolds his arms, reads a few minutes, then stares out to sea with easy motions. I wonder at his beauty and the fluidity of every movement. He effortlessly strikes a painter's pose.

His wife walks up to him. She is dark and brown, with the soft underarms of a middle-aged woman. He looks up and puts his hand on the small of her back.

Tomorrow we travel to the Savonlinna Opera Festival for a weekend of operas in Finland with old family friends, Meg and Herrick Baltschefsky.

July 22

Olavinlinna Castle is a stunning medieval structure built in 1475 and surrounded by water. The stage rests against the side of the castle. The dark gray stone stretches above us, warmed by the colors of the evening sun. The roof is slatted and the sun slants in, throwing thick lines onto the stage. Last night we heard *Aida*. I had forgotten how beautiful the music is. The birds loved it, too, and sang throughout the night until the sun finally set. As we stumbled out at midnight, the moon rose over the lake, full and shimmering.

Meg and Herrick are wonderful to be with. At dinner Herrick is a perfect companion, ordering the wines and dishes. He is partly

Finnish and speaks the odd Slavic-sounding language. Cassie sits with us, a beautiful ten year old. Her clear skin, red mouth, and eyes brim with mischief.

July 23

On the return trip we visit Herrick's cousin, Christer Kihlman, a nationally recognized Finnish writer. Recently appointed permanent residence in Finland's official "writer's house," he moved into the beautiful 1700s stone house with thick walls, white pine floors, and old furniture. I recognize Christer immediately as kindred. We speak of our work, nodding in agreement, knowing exactly what the other means.

Cassie suddenly pipes up. "My mom never has time for me."

Christer studies her gravely for a moment, then nods his head. "Yes, parents and artists don't mix well. They always think of their work." Cassie's face breaks into a smile.

Back in the car, she dozes with her head on my arm, hot and slightly moist. I examine the delicate hairs on her cheek. She knows: To create one must be absent. I tend and nurture my evolving work, minutely stitch and weave sounds together, move energy around, quickening the pace, landing neatly only to push off again. And even when I am with Cassie, I am not always present. Often my gaze is far off; I put her voice on mute.

I am not an inattentive parent, but it is clear I have another life that calls for my attention and drags me under.

July 26

Is my music an attempt to control time? Often it is a passage or a journey, other times a documentation of now. Do I compose to control life or explain it? I have a back and forth, give and take, learning and growing relationship with my work. I dip into a sea of myself and try to capture it in music to share with others. My work and life are fluid and I experience myself through it.

My work has a life of its own and often insists on its own way. But it is reciprocal; as I reveal myself to my music, the music reveals myself to me. The work teaches me where to go and what next to learn.

July 27

"Love shows us ourself, the edge of our lives, what we know and don't know. Desire is what is missing and opens us up to wanting to be whole. Desire changes us. Desire brings absent into present; it is an act of 'now.' Knowing and desiring have the root in the same thing. The people we love are never just as we desire them."[5]

Love shows me what I lack. Like knowledge, love is a desire to extend myself, to go into the unknown with my mind and my heart. It throws me into a now of pleasure and pain, delight and sorrow.

I get snagged on the future of love, what will be. In truth, I will never have what I imagine, because I am always changing. To have what I want is to try to control time. By doing that— paradox of paradoxes—I cannot have my heart's desire: love as it is in the now. My task is to understand the difference between now and then, and keep them separate. It is no surprise that I am confused and wish to merge the two. My beginnings are based on absence. I stepped out of sight and lost Solvig's love.

I stumble on desire and love; I see it in terms of existence.

July 30

The evening is cool after another record hot day. I am awake through the night. We went to Vaxjo where Solvig is buried and Torsten still lives. The cemetery was beautiful, with flowers on every grave, the hedges and grass green despite the dry weather. I stood there, next to Kjell-Olof, remembering. In front of Solvig's tombstone, tears slipped down my cheeks. He held my hand.

I asked Solvig, "Will you love me if I let you go?"

July 31

I sit on the big rock by the lake. The wind is soft on my face, my back is warmed by the sun. Small ducks play submarine. Soon it will be time to leave Sweden and start our last two weeks of travel. I have received what I came for.

Yesterday, I sat at my foster father's table with Cassie curled up in my lap. I listened to my foster family speaking in lilting Swedish and I could almost understand. I listened as if I were three years old, not for content but for inflection. Lulled by the sound, the music of my parents' words.

Torsten is beautiful at eighty years old. His blue eyes are bright, his laughter warm. He speaks almost no English and I no Swedish. I watch his expressions. "It has been many years," he said haltingly, "since you and Kjell-Olof played together." Yes, they translated, in 1956. They laughed about something we used to do.

"You were very..." they conferred, and the word finally came back, "clever."

This is the land of my birth. The dark pine forest, the troll woods, the moss-covered rocks. The rich and deep color speaks to me, and I understand. My body remembers and resonates. I smell the dry grass and listen to the silence. I bend my head to catch the space between when the sound ends and the silence begins—the space between the known and the unknown. Is this where the soul finds safe harbor?

This day, in its cool warmth, is a fine gift. I luxuriate in it. I prolong the pleasure by writing letters. Anders and Cassie play happily, laughing and saying the few words they learned from each other. I am in a place of peace. This now is an endless now.

August 3

A new piece of music stirs within me. I feel it in my stomach. It twists and wrenches. I know it is time to start, but I bargain for a later date. The piece quiets for a moment, then twists again. There is no real latitude in here. It pretends to placate me but ultimately is relentless. I am relieved. Without its insistence, I am lost.

August 4

Semillia besada, writes Barbara Kingsolver, is the seed that got kissed. I am drawn to the words; they evoke a sense of my next piece. I do not know what it will become, but now I must follow to see what comes. Have I not been kissed by Solvig?

"One of those miraculous fruit trees that taps into an invisible view of nurture and bears radiant bushels of plums while the trees around it merely go on living."[6]

Radiant fruit, the one who is blessed.

I am looking to move away from the linearity of my music and explore the circular radiance of joy, or being, a new vision of love and light.

Seeds ripen in their own time, in their own season; their clock answers to no one. The process doesn't exact a price—it merely is. Being blessed has no meaning or specialness other than itself. It merely is. The divine has no price tag.

August 5

A soft rainy day in Oslo, Norway. I'm at a way station between this world and my outward life. Like a deep-sea diver, I must slowly rise to the surface or I will experience the excruciating pain of the bends.

August 6

What is the shape of this new work? How is it different from the shape of other works? Need it be different?

Semillia Besada is the tiny kernel that contains the world. All is ready in an enormous fecundity, the blessedness. Evolved and in a process of revealing the exuberance of being. Chords swell. Density of a seed, a microcosm of the world.

August 7

Rilke keeps speaking to me; his presence and vision deeply resonate with me. I smile as I read his poems. "Singing is Being" (*Gesang ist Dasein*). Filled with understanding, I shudder. To whom will I whisper these heart-things?

My music is the only answer. The aloneness in the presence of the transcendent moment staggers me. There is no relief from the joy or the pain. The moment I begin to feel, the floodgates open.

Be the crystal cup that shattered even as it rang
Be—and yet know the great void where all things begin,
The infinite source of your own most intense vibration,
So that, this once, you may give it your perfect assent.

Joyfully add yourself, and cancel the count.[7]

August 9
We rest in Stockholm for a few days. The tall buildings are softly curved and colored, stately but sumptuous. Gold leaf gleams from cornices, green from copper roofs, and ornate stones decorate the facades. The water glimmers, the sky a blue usually only found on a crisp autumn day. The clouds catch the evening colors as the day begins to close. Tonight we watch fireworks on the dock's edge. The display is spectacular: shooting stars, loud bursts, glittering colors, and fine fairy fingers of light reaching out to us. If we humans can design such wonderful sights, certainly world peace is only a step away.

August 11
On the final leg of our Swedish journey, we are out in Toro again with Meg and Herrick on their little island retreat. After a long hot sauna we swim, our naked bodies green with the color of the Baltic Sea. Later I sit on the rocks. The sky keeps changing in color and clouds, blowing different patterns of blue-violet and blue-grays across the sky. Suddenly a rainbow is iridescent above the skyline.

August 16

Copenhagen and long days of walking around. I tire of this life. The pavements are unrelenting and hard. Cassie dances around me. "I am so happy we are going home on Friday!" she shouts.

August 18

A storm blew in last night, with buckets of rain, thunder, and lightning; in the morning it drizzled. The Little Mermaid statue sits on a large granite stone in the old port district of Nyhavn. In the gray morning light she looks miserable, her legs half fins, half human. My eyes start to fill with tears. "Are you going to cry?" Cassie accuses.

Yet at the Hirschsprung Collection, full of Danish art, I am warmed. I sigh and accept it with delight. I inhale the visions of life, full of color and richness. I stare into the eyes of a person in the portraits. They stare back. They know me.

Tomorrow we return home.

Chapter 17

PORTAL

Kibbutz Magal is located in the Wadi Ara region of the Sharon plain in Israel. I work in the banana plantation, cutting the small shoots from the trees early in the morning. At lunch, we break. The self-serve table in the dining room is piled with tomatoes, cucumbers, peppers, hardboiled eggs, and falafel, balls of deep-fried chickpeas. I ladle out sour cream from a large vat.

In the evening we lounge with young soldiers. They talk loudly, flinging their arms in gestures; the language is harsh and guttural. I am in love with Haim. His family is originally from Yemen. His white teeth glisten against his blue-black skin. When Israel was still Palestine, his father walked barefoot across the desert to find home.

"Are you a virgin?" Haim whispers in my ear.

"No," I lie.

A song breaks out. The women sing earnestly. "Hineh ma tov uma na'im" (how good it is), "shevet achim gam yachad" (to sit here together).

The night is clear. The song lingers in the air.

My mother's appointment to direct the Israeli student exchange program came just as I graduated from high school. In June, she left us at the farm under my father's care, entrusting me with the packing for our year abroad. Deferring college for a year, I was responsible to take the children, my grandmother, and the Dodge van to Israel by ocean liner in August. I was eighteen. Eva was eleven, Scott nine, Lâle seven, and little Loren four. I panicked. "Don't worry," my mother soothed. "Grandma will help."

My mother's mother had lived with us for over ten years, helping care for the household while my mother was at work. The winter before we left for Israel, she had broken her hip on her way to fetch a load of laundry from the basement. Crying out for help, she lay all afternoon on the small landing at the bottom of the stairs. My brother was home from school with a high fever. Stuporous, he followed the sound of her voice to find her with a bone protruding from her flesh. After a long convalescence, Grandma healed, but her mind slipped and wandered. She was in her eighties and less than reliable.

During the summer, my stepfather built large, heavy packing cases out of plywood. I folded clothing, sheets, towels, and blankets. Lining up shoes and boots, I remembered rain jackets and winter coats. I packed tents, sleeping bags, and camping equipment. Books, piano, and violin music piled high; I shopped for school supplies. The kids romped around me, pestered each other. They lay down in the crates and pretended they had died. They packed and unpacked their toys. Loren tried to fit his tricycle in.

In the evenings, my stepfather taught me how to drive. He had an old Opel that routinely fell out of third gear. Carefully double clutching, I held the stick shift in place before shifting into fourth. The gears ground while I practiced. The car lurched. I turned the wrong way. He swore loudly and grabbed the steering wheel with his large hands. His boot stomped on my foot to brake the car.

We had become careful around my stepfather. His irritation and impatience seemed more acute, and his silences deeper. Lâle, sensitive to his shifts in mood, would start to cry. Scott often threw up in the middle of dinner. We stayed out of his way.

Finally it was time to leave. A trailer was hitched onto the back bumper and filled with the heavy crates. I was to drive the Opel, but it had developed more serious problems. It was safer that I drive the van with the trailer. We set out on the nine-hour drive to the New York City harbor. I had just passed my driver's license exam two days before. It was my first solo drive.

Driving in tandem with my stepfather, my grandmother dozed in the passenger seat. My back was covered in sweat. The trailer fishtailed and shuddered. We stopped to get gas. "You are driving too slowly," my stepfather admonished. "We will never make the boat if you don't put on some speed."

I drove as fast as I could. I smiled when I hit sixty miles an hour. The trailer swung gently behind the van; we moved smoothly ahead. Some time later, a car pulled up by my side, honking. It was my stepfather. His face was bright red. He shouted behind the closed car window. My siblings waved frantically. In my speed, I had not noticed that he exited the highway. By the time he realized the mistake and turned around, it took him an hour to catch up with me.

The SS Queen Anna Maria sat in the harbor, an enormous steely tipped vessel. Built in the 1950s, the ship had been recently acquired by the Greek Line. The porters loaded our crates on board and hoisted the van up onto the deck with a large crane. Walking over the narrow gangplank, we made our way to the bottom of the boat, the tourist class. My stepfather gave us a quick hug goodbye. The hallways swam with passengers, suitcases, and trucks. Stewards with piles of towels in their arms zipped and zagged. We were on our own for the next twelve days.

I have only a few memories of our time on board. The ocean was calm, and the days were bright. I herded the kids to the outdoor pool and fed the youngest at the dinner table. When Lâle had a high fever, I cooled her in the shower. When Scott went missing, I found him. And when Eva told me she was molested in the elevator by a dining room waiter that she recognized, I went like an angel of fury to the ship's administration.

The chief purser listened carefully. Lips pressed together, I shook as I spoke. The next day, he brought Eva and me to see the captain. Short and stout, he sat behind a gray marble-topped desk, dressed in the brilliant whites of seamen. A large cigar was between his stubby fingers.

"What happened?" he inquired.

Eva pressed into me. As I began to explain, the door opened and two men brought in the offender. He was small and handsome; he looked down at his hands. Eva turned green and shrank. Without a word, the captain waved them out of the room.

"He is Italian," he said with disgust. "We have to take on workers from every port. This would not have happened if he was Greek!" The waiter would be relieved of his duties and put in the brig. The captain continued talking. His hand gestured, the cigar wafted smoke, the marble table glistened and mirrored his

208

movements. What possessed these men to listen to a teenager and her younger sister?

At long last, we arrived in Haifa. The children and my grandmother went through customs with joyful shouts. I waited for the van and the crates to be offloaded. Hours went by. I talked to my mother through the chain link fence. She passed me food. Finally the crane lowered the van onto the dock. The men unchained the chassis and I jumped in. As I turned the ignition and pressed the accelerator, the gas pedal linkage broke with a loud pop. The car would not move. I burst into tears.

Israel, in 1971, was in a quiet period between the Six-Day War and the Yom Kippur War of 1973. Bordered by hostile countries and the sea, it is barely bigger than New Jersey. A four-hour car ride brings you to Jordan and the Sea of Galilee. A six-hour drive south, and you are at the Suez Canal, Sharm el-Sheikh, and Egypt. Almost straight north is Haifa, Lebanon, and Syria. The modern city of Tel Aviv is an hour away from the ancient city of Jerusalem. There, Jews, Muslims, and Christians sway back and forth on the narrow streets. The Wailing Wall, the Dome of the Rock, and the Church of the Holy Sepulchre.

The language is hard on the ears; Israelis are often loud and rude. "*Slicha*," excuse me, staccatos a woman as she elbows her way past me. On public transportation the driver yells at a passenger. Snapping sunflower seeds between his teeth, he sticks his hand out the side window to gesture rudely to a motorist who has cut him off. "*Lama ma*?" he grimaces. "*Mamzer!*" Bastard! On the streets, soldiers prowl with machine guns. There is a constant, tense vigilance.

We settled in a small house on the outskirts of Tel Aviv. The year was mine, and, as long as I stayed busy with education pursuits, I had few childcare duties. My mother and I enrolled in an Ulpan to learn Hebrew and studied at night with a tutor. I took modern dance classes at the Bat-Dor Dance Company and piano with Professor Klein at the University of Tel Aviv School of Music. I sat in on my mother's class on existentialism and studied sculpture at a local art school.

I practiced the piano every day for hours in the tiled living room. Part sport, part artistry, I learned difficult sections like soccer drills, repeating them over and over again until the fingers mastered the pattern and set it into muscle memory. Playing now in slow motion I could observe the flow: notes moving together as an ensemble, or in opposition for balance. A sour, discordant note made following notes sweeter, and a soaring expansion of sound broke in a tremble of deliciousness.

The house swirled with Bach, Beethoven, and Schumann. Halfway through a long piece, Bach would drop in a two-measure jewel—a complete surprise and surrender—then move on. Why had he not made a whole piece out of this tiny, beautiful phrase? Did he have such abundance in his creative storehouse that he left it there, bare and gleaming, knowing he had plenty more? My chair scraped on the tile floor, and outside on the patio, the bougainvillea hung heavily, a brilliant swatch of crimson.

I knew nothing about Jewish history, culture, or religion—an ironic twist of growing up in a liberal household. I began with a Jewish encyclopedia and quickly moved to books of Jewish history and religion, then Shmuel Yosef Agnon, Isaac Bashevis Singer, and Sholem Aleichem. I fell in love with Martin Buber's translation of the stories of Bal Shem Tov, the gentle, mystical rabbi who founded Hasidic Judaism.

These readings, however, did not help me understand the Israel of contradictions or the sharpness of that time. I understood the watchfulness, even paranoia, hemmed in by dangerous border countries and generations of hostilities toward Jews. But I was dumbfounded by the prejudice toward Sephardic Jews and could not balance the displacement of the Palestinians and Bedouins, who also lived on holy ground.

By spring, I had spent a week in Sinai, visited Masada and Qumran in the Negev Desert, and come out of the Dead Sea coated with a layer of thick salt. I hitchhiked or caught rides with friends or family to the Sea of Galilee, Nazareth, Bethlehem, Eilat, Golan Heights, and Jericho. I worked at the Miles Laboratory as a lab technician and spent a month farming at Kibbutz Magal. In between, I fell in love with a pianist. He did not return my affection.

The year passed quickly, joyfully. I loafed, I dreamed, I wrote poetry. I found I loved to learn and that I could be independent. Through the portal of Israel, a land of contrast, spirituality, and violence—of questions that had no discernible answers—I passed, finally, out of my childhood.

Chapter 18

A DIFFERENT TRUST

Philadelphia (1994)

The true meaning of life is to plant trees, under whose shade you do not expect to sit.

Nelson Henderson

August 30

It is early in the morning, and for the first time since our return from Sweden, I have pen in hand. The trip home was uneventful, and we unpacked quickly, finding places for our treasures. Cassie left for her father's, and then I worked ten hours a day for nine days completing the parts to my orchestra piece. After a final proofing, the piece goes to the printers.

I drive down to the shore for a final summer weekend. I have not lost Sweden yet. I feel open to the world. The evening is beautiful after a day of gray skies and rain in Mantoloking. The sea, reflecting the pink glowing clouds, cuts through my body. I stand, bare feet in cold sand. My brother Scott leans handsome against the water. The dog frisks wildly.

August 31

My dreams are full of earthquakes, and I wake thinking of my upcoming three-year residency.

My Meet the Composer residency is their first national residency that works directly with a social service agency and whose focus is music in the community. With my three host organizations, OperaDelaware, Newark Symphony, and the YWCA, my goal is to demystify the role of the composer and bring community into the creative process. Over the three years, I will write a major work for each of the organizations, as well as work weekly with homeless women at the YWCA shelter and help them write their own opera of their lives.

As the start of the residency nears, I feel a growing sense of responsibility and need to reexamine my commitment. I will have to put aside my quiet composing life and learn a different way of looking at my profession and the way I compose.

The next three years are growth years, seedling years, sowing years. My composing may be secondary to the learning I commit myself to. Heart work in the outside world.

September 2

Summer's end. Early morning I burrow deep in bed under snug blankets. The birds cavort on the lawn, dancing after some bug. The beach is cold and I walk alone.

For the moment, I hold on to this quiet, contemplative life. I fear being lost in the roar of the coming residency. And I welcome it—these eternal paradoxes.

Tonight I will dine with friends. I will wear my lovely green dress and my new silky sweater.

September 11

I spend the whole day making room for the residency in my

studio. I clean out the old material, rearrange, store my completed pencil scores and materials. My desk paperwork is filed, and letters are answered.

In my bright studio, I sit for the first time since the summer travel. A new piece is starting to emerge like a sky spirit. It weaves around my head, barely touching my face, whispering. I am happy to know her, happy she is here.

September 12

Today is the first workday of the residency. I quickly experience how frayed I can become. With the increased demand for my attention, I reconsider everything I do. A few commitments keep me safe. Mornings are devoted to composing. I start the day with an hour of journaling and reading, then move to my composing desk and piano. No phone calls until noon. All residency administrative work starts after lunch. The afterschool care I have carefully constructed for Cassie will allow me time until dinner.

I feel my energy surge. The recording of my ensemble works gets off the ground. I will line up performers and work out the budget. The Cassatt String Quartet project requires effort. I must finalize the project plan for my current residency.

For dinner I eat mussels and read Rilke. Stephen Mitchell's translations are stunning. The long introduction by Robert Haas radiates kindness, understanding, and joy in the poet. I am in the middle of the *Sonnets to Orpheus* and have dared to start the *Duino Elegies*. The words glide through me like music. I hear and feel the poems, but can't grasp onto them.

September 13
I have to laugh at myself. So soon after the calm of yesterday, all is upset. The day stretches out in front of me, and I am unable to work. Metal groans on metal. I connect with my work and disconnect with my life. Always this tension: I want to write a new piece, and I do not want to write a new piece.

September 28
I consider the interval of a fifth and wonder what is at the edge of sound. The fifth is a magic interval, circular and round, empty and full. It has an eerie hollowness to it. I am reminded of the soul. Without having actual form or substance, it is the heart of existence.

I read Rilke every morning. I do not struggle, and I continue to delight in knowing both what I know and do not know. There is something in his poetry that connects deeply with my music— the "Singing is Being." It is enough just to be. To vibrate is to exist. To exult, blossom, to lift one's face up to the sky and roar for joy—that is life. Rilke knows about the experience of ecstasy.

I dig deep, like a rodent burrowing for treasure in the earth of my own soul. I find jewels of inestimable value. I am not special. All of us have deeply buried understandings.

September 30
I dreamed darkly last night and woke up to think of purification. Perhaps I need to forgive myself. What if I treated myself as if I were my dearest beloved child? Would I not be as compassionate as I am to my daughter? I will begin with a *Descanso*—a small memorial so often seen on the side of the road in Mexico. I will

216

decorate with plastic flowers, candles, and a milky white cross; I will mark this change, this turning point.

October 10

I have many meetings with my residency hosts. I am learning quickly to ask questions and to listen. What do you need? What do you want? Here are my talents, how can I serve you?

October 14

I meet with orchestra conductors and I am puzzled. Why is there so little interest in or enthusiasm for new music? Modern dance concerts are brimming with expectant audiences, we run to the bookstore for the latest novel reviewed by the *New York Times*, but an orchestra performs a large new work to a hall that is half empty.

Much blame is due to the orchestras themselves. Fearful of losing their older audiences, they program as if we lived a hundred years ago, playing the classical music with scant attention to new works—as if all the masterpieces were already written. They do not reinvest in music as a living tradition, spending almost no funding—research and development—for new works.

Imagine running to the bookstore eager for the newest novel of John Updike, Joyce Carol Oates, or Michael Ondaatje and finding all the shelves were stacked with Tolstoy and Dickens.

"I'm sorry," says the owner. "We simply do not have anything from the twenty-first century. We did have one copy of Virginia Woolf, but..." His voice trails off. "That was sold a month ago."

October 17

Life continues at its own pace, evolving slowly, moving back and forth like a sensuous slug. There are few abrupt shifts in direction, few sudden turnabouts. I wait for change.

Last night I participated in a guided improvisational evening of dance. I am paired with a bearded, pot-bellied man I do not know, who leaps over and about me, whirling his male body around. I had to smile at this burly, bear-like man; I enjoy his feral freeness. In the final exercises, I closed my eyes. He stood me up and posed me for a tango. Ridiculous, wonderful, and terrifying all at the same time.

October 17

The Orchestra Society of Philadelphia finally performed my saxophone concerto, *Blessings (Sacred Space)*. The concert had been canceled last year when the blizzard hit. It was wonderful to hear the piece; the metallic whining and improvisatory section moved swiftly into the heart of rhythm and melody.

Marshall Taylor, the saxophonist, is a wonderful musician. He captures life in one single note. Nothing is held in reserve. He laughs as he tells me that genius can do anything, but talent can only do one thing. "I'm not good enough to play in an orchestra," he said. "I can only be a soloist." I nod.

Many composers can write in a variety of styles of music. I can only write in my own. Compared to them, I am the dumb kid in the class. Whether my music will last into time, I have no opinion. It is the only music I am capable of writing.

October 28

There is much to be done. I crash from one narrow escape to another. The piece for the opening of the Woman's Resource Center at the YWCA is complete, and I put together the parts. I assemble a portion of the score for framing, a gift to the center.

Tomorrow is a full day of reviewing scores for an upcoming panel session. I farm out Cassie to family friends. On Sunday, I will host a Halloween party for her and a dozen of her school friends.

A year ago I led a solitary life of writing at home, with long evenings of loneliness. This year, the outwardness of the residency already tires me.

October 31

Halloween tricks and treats are in bed. I sit and write, listening to the crickets. Are the cicadas now all dead?

November 8

In the spring, I will teach fifth-grade children in a local public school. How do I teach them to compose music?

Traditionally, one first studies an instrument for years. This is followed by more years of harmony, theory, and counterpoint. Then, and only if you are "talented enough," are you allowed to study composition.

I, however, want to teach composition the way I learned to paint. Walking into my kindergarten class, I see a small easel in the corner with a few paints. My teacher puts a smock on me and then gives me my first art lesson—perhaps the best one in the world. "Try," she says quietly, "not to get the paint on the floor."

Then I paint, and the whole world opens up.

November 15
I rework *Semillia Besada* for double wind quintet and piano. I find it difficult to rethink or expand the piece—as if its shape is immutable. The work does not please me and seems insubstantial. Perhaps I made too many compromises to meet the deadline. I bridged some new material and strayed on shaky ground.

November 28
Four-year anniversary of my heart operation. This is a joyous, albeit slightly anxious anniversary. Here I am, life renewed. A Lazarus walking out of the bowels of the earth.

December 3
I dig into this piece. The structure and discipline of my life while composing is a primordial glue that keeps me from falling apart. Without it, a straight cut through would cause me to fall in two like a neatly sectioned apple.

I am so deep into this new work that life is not a conscious act. Instead, it revolves around me on its own, as if it knows what to do without my directions.

Life is something else; it has a pulse and a rhythm of its own, color and speed. My work is silent, far away, full of itself and only itself. It has my total attention. I am rapt and inert. Then life tugs at me like a suture on the skin. I am willing to leave; this will await me tomorrow when I take up the pencil again.

December 13
Today I feel the pinch of time and focus. I am adrift. The residency adds a measure of confusion to my life.

I continue to reassess who is involved in the first creative process of making music, that of composing. All of us have painted and written poetry, many of us have played an instrument, but few of us have composed music.

Perhaps the estrangement the public has with new music is partly due to this total lack of creative experience. We have developed what I call a "not me" attitude, which has issues of power interlaced in it. In other words, "You have music; I don't. But who cares, because it is not me."

December 15

The Meet the Composer residency continues to go well. I travel down to Delaware several days a week to work with my three hosts. Other than writing music for each of them, I find ways for everyone, regardless of experience, to compose.

Each Monday I work with the residents who live in the YWCA shelter facility for women and their families. I am teamed with writer and director Zadia Ife, who runs the IYABO program, a parenting skills class. She is lovely and thin, and suffers from a chronic illness that often leaves her exhausted, sometimes for days. I know firsthand the carefulness with which she leads her life. We go out to lunch; she has forgotten her coat. She stops and silently calculates how much energy it would cost to run back. She shivers all through lunch.

We meet with the homeless women in the shelter in the evenings. Sitting in a circle in the large blue-tiled kitchen, I am quiet during the first couple weeks and feel my privilege with embarrassment. I am a total novice. Under Zadia's guidance, I begin to learn. I use her credibility to gain admittance into this world; she is my access card.

The women in the residence are kind to me, and slowly over the weeks, we get to know each other. They tell stories of poverty, child abuse, beatings, and addictions. Many of them have lost their children to foster care. All are homeless. I lead a meditation to help them reconnect with their stories. We close our eyes and go back to the house of our childhood. "Listen," I tell them. "What do the walls remember?" Memories emerge, triggered by a door, a closet, or a heating grate.

We begin to create a performance piece they call *Redemption Song*. They will perform it next year at the Jesus Be Ready Church. Taking down the pots and pans of the kitchen, we make a drum circle. Laughing, singing, and sometimes crying, they create a small opera of their stories, their songs—their sorrows and joys, their hopes and desires for a new life.

December 18

I have passed into a different time, a different trust. The inner sadness, fear, and longing have transformed; I have moved on. I have been able to put my old self aside. I occasionally feel the longing, but more often I am seamless and clear.

I am in the middle of a time where there is only composing and teaching. The impulse to create is to transform my life into sound, into breath. Teaching, or connecting with others around music, has become sacred, vital, and moist.

How do I sit today, wide-eyed with full pleasure, and speak of transformation? Nothing and everything have changed. Blessing, clarification, and emerging from the elemental fires have no reason for being; they merely are.

I have no plans but today's plans. I place my hands on my

life, and the roar is suddenly quieted. I am in still waters. I trust that what I do is important and relevant. I give up nothing. The longing and grief have not been lost, but changed, reworked, and remolded. I am no longer a servant and unhappy companion.

I am in the stream of my own life. Humbled, as if I stand in front of a larger presence. I cast my eyes downward. I am supplicant to what is. Am I experiencing the God inside of me, the divine that rests in all of us? I am mute before this beauty and greatness of life. It is astounding and brilliant.

December 23
Christmas Eve. I light candles and ask for Christmas blessings. May I be at peace. May I have clarity. May I experience my life's pain without being controlled by it. May I answer the call to combine a spiritual understanding with my music, to integrate what I know and what I don't know. To dig deeper. To express my life's passion, grief, and joy.

"Shatter my heart so a new room can be built for a limitless love."[1]

Chapter 19

FALLING OFF
THE CLIFF

I slump at the piano. My teacher, Lionel Nowak, leans on the arms of his chair in the corner of his studio. We are silent together. He is a legendary piano teacher at Bennington College, and I am in my first semester as a freshman.

Before me is a Chopin Waltz. I have played well but somehow missed the mark. He peers at me, his thick-rimmed glasses slipping down his nose. "More expression!" he remonstrates. "It's a Romantic piece—play large!"

But I don't want to overdo it and be sentimental, I explain. I was being careful.

"Ah," he chuckles to himself, glancing out the window, "you've got to fall off the cliff a couple times to find out where the edge is!"

❧

By the time I arrived at Bennington College in 1972, I had never written a note of music. In fact, I had never played or heard any music by women composers. It never occurred to me that women could compose.

Bennington, nestled at the foot of the beautiful Vermont Green Mountains, was the first college to include the visual and performing arts as an equal partner in the liberal arts curriculum. The college was well known as one of the most progressive liberal arts colleges; all classes at that time were pass-fail with minimal course requirements. I wasn't sure what I wanted from my college experience other than to immerse myself completely in learning. My mother determined I would be a piano teacher, but I wanted something more.

Music activity at the college was located at Jennings, a stately gray stone manor that had been converted into the music building. It sat on top of a small hill, above a meadow in the back of campus, with practice rooms on the third floor.

The music department boasted of many fine instrumentalists and four composers on their faculty—Louis Calabro, Vivian Fine, Lionel Nowak, and Henry Brant. They believed that all performers should be composers and all composers performers. Moreover, they eschewed the academic approach to composition that prescribed years of study of harmony and theory before you touched pencil to paper. They saw no need to waste precious class time with something you could teach yourself and preferred to teach composition by allowing their students to write music and learn from the performance of it.

My freshman music class was held in Lou Calabro's studio, a large shaded room with velvet sofas and a grand piano overlooking the garden. Lou, a loose-limbed man with a slight stoop and a strong New York accent, was quick to give us our first assignment, to write a duet for two of our classmates. There was little instruction on how to compose. Staff paper was handed out.

I was distinctly grumpy and muttered something about how all good music had already been written and all good composers were dead. But I wrote a piece for oboe and French horn. Twelve measures.

The piece was terrible, and the instrumentalists complained bitterly about the scattered notation and lack of dynamics. I vowed never to write for that combination again. But I was interested and continued composing for my classmates. I wrote a piece for percussion, another for cello, a fugue for the piano.

By the end of my first semester, I was hooked. I decided to use the non-resident term (NRT), a nine-week period between semesters, to compose music. NRT was specifically set aside for students to get work experience, confidence, and practical knowledge in their chosen fields; only seniors were only allowed to use the time for independent study. I needed special permission.

I sat opposite the director of the program while she read my NRT application. She looked at me severely across the desk.

"You are a freshman," she said. "Freshmen do not qualify for special projects."

I clutched onto one rule that Bennington always seemed to honor: If a rule does not fit you, make a strong case for yourself. I seized the opportunity and expressed my newly found passion for composing.

"You know…" She relaxed a bit. "You will have to compose eight hours a day, just like a job."

I nodded.

"And bring back a stack of scores for your teacher to review."

I smiled.

I spent the NRT at the farm in Pittsburgh with my stepfather, composing on the old Fisher grand piano wedged in his tiny front room. The winter was mild, and while he taught during the day, I composed, taking breaks to walk with our large dog, Lord Lovell, through the bare-limbed orchard and over fields of yellow grass.

Winter had softened my stepfather. In the evenings, he read newspapers or magazines, carefully cutting out articles to save. He watered his many plants that blocked most of the sunlight and endlessly cleaned his pipe. Still silent much of the time, I began to enjoy our long quiet meals.

Returning to Bennington in the spring, I knew what I wanted to do in life. It was as if, looking out into the forest, I could see many different paths, but only one was illuminated. More than that, I wanted to know who I was, and composing music was a way of finding out without revealing too much. It was a place of investigation and anonymity.

The years at Bennington passed quickly. Tuesday afternoons the entire music department gathered and played all the music composed that week. Wednesday night was the weekly concert. I studied with witty and generous Vivian Fine, a former student of Ruth Crawford Seeger, and with iconoclast Henry Brant, famous for his acoustic spatial music. He was small, brown, and never without a cap or sunshade on his head. Because he was opinionated and sometimes difficult to study with, I asked him to be my adviser and surreptitiously brought him my scores to look at. His rules for orchestration were brilliant; I still review his notes carefully before I begin a new orchestra piece.

In addition to a full load of music, I studied philosophy, women's studies, and German, and sat in on classes I could not fit in my schedule. On campus were rogue, sharp-tongued Camille Paglia, jazz musicians Bill Dixon and Milford Graves, novelist

Nicholas Delbanco, and Alan Cheuse, who later became a long-time literary commentator for NPR. John Gardner arrived on campus in 1974 shortly after the publication of his novel *Grendel*. Sporting long white hair and a pipe, he made a regular appearance at the music department concerts.

I learned to play viola, then cello. With friends, I was the harpsichordist for an early music group we called Plumb Baroque. Evenings were spent in Jennings playing piano four-hands late at night with my friend Beth. Her little hands flashed next to mine as we sight-read all the string quartets of Beethoven and the symphonies of Mozart. On weekends I caught up on my studies and cleaned houses in town, staffed the music library, or copied teachers' scores on the old Bruning machine in the basement of the music building.

As composing became my voice, piano was my anchor. My teacher, Lionel Nowak, was well known for having been the Music Director of the Humphrey-Weidman Dance Company, composing ballet scores for choreographer José Limón before coming to Bennington. Tall and often dressed in a light blue shirt, he was an imposing, revered presence who spoke sparingly and rarely gave compliments. He was adored by all.

At lessons, he listened intently with his eyes closed. "Get into the piano keys, like clay," he would say, lifting his head and waving one hand. "Dig deep into them—don't be afraid. Don't back away from anything."

"Courage!" He sat rumpled in the chair, his right index finger raised. "You must always dare to make a fool of yourself, and then you'll be able to do things you never dreamed you could."

He shrugged his shoulders. "Learn to be embarrassed."

In the summer of my sophomore year, I traveled to Sweden for the first time since my birth. Two months later I returned with the knowledge that my mother was not my adoptive mother but my birth mother.

I spent a week at home before I dared say anything to my mother. On a hot day in August, I took her to the park near our house. We sat at a picnic table, in the shade of a patch of giant pines. The tall trunks stood close together, with the tops almost out of sight, bending with a slight breeze. I revealed what I had learned.

"I meant to tell you." She reached for my hand over the table and began to cry. I looked at her quietly. Her tears were of a lost love, a lost life—a fairy-tale life snatched out of her grasp. Heartsick in Sweden, little Tina had saved her, brought meaning back into her life. She kept this love hidden, this terrible stab to her heart.

"How could you have waited so long to tell me?" I asked.

"It's my story!" she snapped. "And I had to protect myself." She feared she would lose her job and standing if others knew she had a child out of wedlock.

The pines stirred. "Does Dad know?" I asked. She squeezed my hand tighter. She would tell my stepfather, but I had to promise not to tell my siblings, at least not right away.

Later I received a rare phone call from my stepfather. "She told me," he said flatly. He was angry. He felt betrayed. Always suspecting, he asked her once in the first year of their marriage. She was not ready to talk about it yet. He waited and never asked again.

I held my breath; my eyes stung.

I returned to college with this amazing and terrible information undigested and promptly fell in love. He was a fellow composer, a year my senior, blond, blue-eyed, and as serious about composing as I was. We became inseparable, going up to Jennings in the early morning and returning late at night. He wrote a set of piano pieces for me; I listened to him play the Fender bass in his band.

Love, however, did not open me to joy but instead to a sharp craving. It was a dark, underground stream of feelings I did not understand. Being with him woke in me a voracious longing that had no name. I was testy, bleak, and many times unbalanced.

As he prepared to leave for graduate school, he broke off our relationship. I fell into a depression so deep that no memory remains of the following nine months. Breathing was difficult and sleep was not refreshing. It was a darkness with no bottom. I recognized this emptiness; it had touched the edges of my childhood, sat with me as a teenager. It now had widened and enveloped me.

I flung myself into my final year of college with manic ferocity. I composed and conducted my first orchestra piece for the local Sage City Symphony. I gave a concert of piano music written for children, including Ernest Bloch's *Enfantines* and Lou Calabro's *Five for a Nickel Pie*. For my spring senior concert I learned Bach's *English Suite* and several of Debussy's *Images*, including the ethereal *Reflets dans l'eau*. I wrote a large ensemble piece with home-made percussion and chimes from plumbing pipes.

Graduation came. I packed. I was ready to move forward.

Bennington College was, in the end, seminal in my development as a musician and composer. The faculty did not teach me how to write music; instead, they invited me in joyfully and with generosity. They fostered inclusion—everyone was worthy of this particular creative process, from bright-eyed beginners to sullen veterans. They believed learning was doing, again and again.

They taught me the difference between criticism and critical thinking. The former takes a stance of superiority, the latter is respectful and self-questioning—what works or doesn't, and how can I do better next time.

They were at the heart of artistic endeavor—bold, generous, humorous, and supportive. They taught me as a fellow composer and musician, one of their tribe.

Chapter 20

DECAY

Philadelphia (1995)

Peace I leave with you, my peace I give to you. I do not give to you as the world gives. Do not let your hearts be troubled and do not be afraid.

You have heard me say, "I am going away and I am coming back to you."

John 14: 25, 28

January 10

The days are calm and steady. The work on the residency goes well, with new plans and ideas of connecting with others in the field.

My cousin Hank died recently of AIDS. His parents are among my favorite relatives, and I am deeply sad.

January 24

Roanoke Symphony premiered *They Come Dancing*. I was overjoyed with the performance; the piece is substantial and full of dance.

Dance is sacred. Certain rhythms cannot be understood with the mind, only felt by the body. I am at the mercy of a deep body wisdom. Movement honors the curves and thighs, celebrates the physical realm. "Isn't this body amazing, a miracle?" I cry out, "See how beautiful I am, how gleaming, how voluptuous!" I am no longer the dancer but the dance, and finally, just the movement.

January 28

Hank stays on my mind. His story and my aunt's grief weigh on me. She went to San Francisco to care for him in the many months he lay ill and dying.

February 4

Midnight. Cassie sleeps upstairs while the first snow of winter softly shrouds the city. The quiet is contagious. No cars are out, an empty trolley ghosts silently by. The snow is steady and white, the sky is filled with the reddish-orange of reflected city lights. I have felt, in the last few days, an unexpected pleasure in being alive. No particular reason, just a steady calm and peaceful joy of living. The work goes well but not spectacularly.

I have been reading John Hull's *Touching the Rock*, an account of gradually losing eyesight as an adult. Finally, after five years of blindness, he even loses the image of his loved ones in his mind's eye. In this dark place, a state of "deep blindness," there is a miraculous change.

"One must recreate one's life or be destroyed," he writes.

Blindness becomes a "dark, paradoxical gift" that helps him create himself anew. "For most of the time now," he continues, "my brain no longer hurts with the pain of blindness."

February 6

Oh, old boyfriends! He is beautiful tonight, with a glowing face, calm and centered. We eat together in a steamy little restaurant in South Philly. I think, "Be present in this moment."

I touch his cheek, he kisses my hand.

February 8

My heart often hurts with being single. Moving into an unpaired state is a startling change and loss of what was hoped to be. While it may not be a life sentence, a reprieve cannot be foretold. I must live as if it will never happen, otherwise, I partner with longing. To enjoy what I have, I give up the past reality and future thinking; I recreate myself.

Being single is a savoring of the silence of the day and the space in my bed. I rely on a deeper sense of inner life. Having no one to talk to in the middle of the night, I write in my journal late, turning an idea 'round in my mind. Longing for companionship, I grow to be a better companion to myself. Missing a shared life, I reflect myself deeply in my work. Yearning for sexual fulfillment, I please myself.

February 13

I read an article about Tchaikovsky's homosexuality and whether he projected his shame onto his music. The author argues that we put meaning on his life that may not be there. Homosexuality in Russia during the 1840s was fairly common and Tchaikovsky, possibly, had little shame about it. Tchaikovsky's diaries are cryptic; he writes that he indulged in "z" or "x"—possibly homosexual relations or, gambling, which Tchaikovsky did at some loss to himself.

We want so to attach meaning, to understand, to pin the moment down when it is, at best, a transitory happening. My journals, for example, are an outpouring of the difficulties and pain I feel in my life. But the pain does not possess me in the way the journals seem to indicate. I work, I compose, I care for Cassie; I am happy and joyous. My journals are truthful and honest, but they are only intermittently accurate.

My music, which contains me, is also not accurate. There is something else, something I cannot get my tongue around. I bend forward and listen to a recording of one of my pieces, trying to understand. It is massive and powerful and full of feeling. I wrote it but do not recognize myself. The work is myself in the future, the vision I have of myself and the world to come. I recognize only that it emanates from my core and continues to a place I do not know.

Something happens when I compose that, for all my self-analysis and precious rethinking, I have no control over. The work is larger than me, and now completed I cannot imagine how I wrote it, or even have much memory of having done so. I am not saying that something took over me and wrote the music, or that I don't remember the content. But in the journey of composing, I go to a place that transforms the work into more than me.

What can it be? Second sight, intuition, a deep understanding that goes beyond the mind and ability to understand? Perhaps it is a primal knowing of the Earth's center, massive movements of the rocks, a slipping and sliding of the sun, ribbons of light. I struggle to discover myself, but this is a place I will never know with my mind. Only through my touch, my hearing—through the beating of my heart.

February 15

In the music world, it is a Promethean activity to allow just *anyone* to write music. Ownership is hotly contested. At a recent concert, a composition faculty member of a prestigious university approached me. We spoke of the work I am doing in Delaware, teaching non-musicians to compose. He was quiet and somber.

Finally he said, "I prefer to bring people *into* the mystery of music, not demystify it."

I prefer the door to be open to all.

March 1

Finally March, the tiebreaker to winter's hold. I am in a hormonal swing. My breasts are tender, my body is sluggish, waiting for the tide to break. Always an odd time of the month, this filling up and emptying out, a stillness between the two.

I am finishing the solo voice and chorus piece for the YWCA. The work goes smoothly but not ecstatically. I go to sleep early, happy to close my eyes to the gray weather.

March 18

There is no question that I love a good drama. I was both born an artist and groomed as one by circumstance. My task is both to experience my life and be a stern guardian over the actresses who would dearly love to "do the scene." A strength and a weakness; I am willing to step into the arena and submit myself to the passion of the moment. At the same time, I indulge myself, wring my hands, and throw myself about. These two determined halves sway back and forth, verging on crisis and pulling back.

This cannot be easy on my friends. They are the gentle and firm hands that help me as I spin off in real pain or assumed posture. They must tire of my repeated bouts of drama. "Won't she just get on with it?" I imagine them asking.

Yet they also know each time is a new awareness. Growth and change are circuitous and rarely swift. Patiently, they reel me back in, as if I were a kite on a long string caught by a wind and dashing myself by swooping and spinning. Hand over hand they tow me to where a good steady breeze catches me. I am on my own again.

Drama serves me well in music. I have an unerring ability to sniff out and articulate the amplification of feelings. I know how to focus tension and release, to pay out the line in a melody or a rhythmic section just so much before snapping it back. The music moves along, glowing in energy and intensity, then suddenly is someplace else. The listener is startled for a moment but recognizes it as exactly and unpredictably right. The transition, the heightened intensity, and the resolution feel where they should be.

Tonight I light candles. The Third Turning:
first you turn in grief,
then you turn in joy.
finally you turn in divinity.

April 1
We are up in the beautiful Pennsylvania Endless Mountains. The cabin is nestled by the woods; a brook trickles by; we are surrounded by faint green fields. Cassie and I walk in the cool of the spring day, collecting bones and looking for wildflowers. The dog bounces around us. She runs through the dark fir trees laughing. In the late afternoon, I nap in the quiet of the house. The candles are lit; dinner is chopped and ready to cook. The dog sleeps at my feet.

April 12
I teach my first Young Composer program to fifth graders. This school is in an economically depressed section of town, and many

of the kids are at risk. Looking around the classroom I see garbage cans, desks, and chairs; we begin a drum circle. We walk around the room with chopsticks to find the best sound in the room. We catalog all the sounds our body can make: teeth chattering, snorts, finger snaps, and thigh slaps. One of the boys turns red as he makes a rude noise.

At the end of the class I ask, "What do you have at home that you can bring in to make instruments?"

"Junk," they yell back. And they bring what they have from their recycling bins: A shoebox becomes a guitar, tin cans become drums, and plastic soda bottles become shakers decorated with strings of beads. Suddenly they can't wait to write music.

We begin with graphic notation—drawing the sound on large paper, where the shape and density of the mark indicate pitch. Then, reducing the paper, they compose with invented notation—looking at how long a sound lasts (duration) and how the sound moves up and down (pitch). And always as a gift; they write pieces to share in performance with others.

The classroom is filled with sound. Children run back and forth conferring with each other. I am swarmed and surrounded. They press up at me, their faces bright. "Miss Tina?" They tug at me. "Let me play you my music."

May 9

These have been good months for me, full of life, work, family, friends, and fun—the fruit of accepting my connection to others. I feel the abundance of my life instead of the few things I lack. The residency continues to be rich, but I have lost some of the focus on my work. I am not worse off because of it, but I am writing differently. Always the flow of learning and the sway from one side to the other.

May 14

I am writing two of the songs for my new opera, "Wedding Song" and "Passage." Eva's lyrics are wonderful and the pieces are going well. I feel there is a new softness and clarity in my work. As I begin to hear this piece, I am struck by the perfection of choosing the string quartet as ensemble for the opera. It allows me latitude and flexibility between the *Billy and Zelda* stories. The vocal writing will be straightforward, leaving the complexities for the string writing.

June 3

If only I could read my life as a story instead of living it! The reader, by now, would be exhausted by the length of this loneliness.

"Is she still lonely?" she'd ask, frowning a bit. "Why doesn't she just find a lover, or get on with it if none is available?" She thumbs through the next few pages. Again, lonely in the chapter ahead. "How could she still be caught up in this? Doesn't she have any pride?" Frustrated, she flips to the final chapters and arrives at what takes years in real life. "Finally, she finds peace. At last."

In a story, I'd skip the loneliness. In a story, I'd stop thinking and it would cease to be. But in life, I am forced to live one day followed by the next. There is no sudden mercy. While I love my life now, without a husband, a single parent, a working artist—don't think for a minute that the nights are not long. I struggle where I am, take the time needed, and pray that the dissatisfaction will not diminish the sweetness of the joy.

June 16

I am leaving for a two-week stay in Utah. There is something new in the air, a new understanding. Ease my way? No, I don't think so. It is time to shatter what I know and restructure it based on new learning. I send out prayers for strong sight.

June 17

The drive down from Salt Lake City to Springdale is beautiful. The landscape opens up, each turn a new vista, dark mountains, sudden sunlight, rain, then an open green plain. I speed along like a racer in a movie. Today is cool. My artist friend Vicki and I camp outside of Zion next to a rapidly rushing river. It roars all night long.

June 18

The mountains of Zion National Park are granite slabs of stone with rich dark reds and sometimes yellow-white. In the afternoon I hike alone to the Court of the Patriarchs while Vicki paints. The horse trail leads into the hot sand terrain of these mountains, which stand tall, massive, and blood red. Coming to the Streaked Wall, I sit for a long time. The immovable passage of time, where the cycles of life are so much longer than ours. The enormous walls of white stone are slightly concave with long streaks, a weeping mountain.

What is it about death that follows me about? At the beautiful emerald pools, a waterfall juts out over the high overhanging ledge. As I rest, three little Mormon girls, in long Sunday dresses and shiny black pumps, arrive. They clatter along the edge; their heels skid and slide around on the rocks near the precipice. I have to turn away. How many slip to their death? How many reckless youths stray just a little too far?

241

June 19

At Bryce Canyon I am moody and quiet. I chafe the way the landscape chafes. A landscape devolving, bare ruined choirs. Where Zion stands tall and impenetrable, like bowels of the earth, Bryce reveals how tenuous the hold can be and crumbles into the canyon below. The day is brilliant with a blue sky and hot sun. We look out at the delicate pinnacles that are shaped by water and wind erosion. It is a landscape being reclaimed.

June 20

At the campsite I pick up my phone messages. Muneko from the Cassatt Quartet has terrible news: Anna, the cellist, is diagnosed with tongue and neck cancer. Beautiful, long-haired Anna, only thirty-two. She recorded my string quartet *Cassandra Sings* and played the long cello introduction with passion and strength.

Death again. Hank and the new orchestra piece dedicated to his life rests continually in my mind. I just finished reading Paul Monette's *Last Watch of the Night,* a tender tribute to dying with AIDS.

What am I here to learn? But perhaps that is just it. I want there to be a meaning, and that is precisely what there is so little of. These deaths or illnesses or losses or joys make no sense—there is only this permanence of stone, these massive warriors of the earth's song.

Anna, Anna! How will I stand by you and send you blessings for healing? Last night I dreamed we were turning into lizards. First our hands, the thumb and forefinger turning scaly green and gray. What is the wisdom of the crone, what do my inner sources know? Lizards are sentinels, their ancestors go way back.

June 22

I finger dinosaur bones. The store on Utah Route 24 is filled with hundreds of them, cut and polished to reveal the silica that seeped into the dinosaurs as they lay buried. Life turned into jewels.

The owner watches me. "You better be careful, or you'll get bone fever!" his voice crackles.

The fossilized bones are dark, the marrows and cells gleam with color and sparkle. I press their coolness to my cheek. So, is that it? Our remains turn to beautiful delicate jewels in the millenniums to come? I do not understand. I wait and dream.

June 22

Midsummer and now the light grows shorter. Author Gretel Ehrlich writes, "The landscape changes, fall to winter, winter to spring, suffering its own terminal disease in such a way that I know nothing is unseasonable, no death unnatural."[1]

Arches National Park is a perfect combination of Bryce and Zion. The tall, massive red rocks break down into rubble, but slowly. Bryce is badlands, where a man builds his house on sand. Corruption comes swift, the death of a landscape, the reclaiming of the mountains by wind and rain. And my cousin Hank—was he reclaimed?

Sometimes I almost grasp an enormous carpet. I cannot see the great design of the carpet, the beautiful material it is made of, the craft, or the time of its making. I hold tightly to the small piece in my hand and guess at the rest.

This is the carpet of connection where nothing is out of place. Grief, pain, destruction, and violation just are; beauty, joy, and love just are. I feel with a passive openness that neither resists nor closes off. I do not understand as much as I connect. I do not know as much as I feel.

The Fisher Towers are beyond words. The canyon was created by silts from flood waters being laid on salt flats. As the water eroded the salt, the earth gave way, eventually forming these large, thin drip castles, slender and tall.

I walk the two-mile trail back along the towers. The enormous dissolving clay structures throw huge cool shadows. As if molded out of hunks of clay, the surface is smeared with a potter's slip, oozing and slopping in piles.

I am alone on the trail, and I use both my body and mind to find the path marked by small cairns. Sometimes the path disappears altogether. I stop, go back a few paces, and search the rocks for signs of a path. I start up again.

The balance between the mind and the body is wonderful. The body, full of itself, negotiates inclines and rocks, assesses the need for water and shade. The mind, busy with inner voices, stays alert to the path and hidden cairns. I am both present and absent. As the body works, I take in the landscape, reflect on the things I am to learn, and find my way.

June 24

Our last few days in the west. New meanings unfold but never where I expect them. Many times it is only the act of seeking and watching, without knowing really what I need. I am a lizard on the sunny side of the rock's crest.

Death and limitation have been the constant on this trip. The landscape, massive and beyond the mind's ability to take in, is deteriorating and dissolving on a daily basis. My cousin is dead and Anna sickens. Beauty around me is constantly reabsorbed and redefined.

It is glib to say we value life because there is death, or beauty because there is ugliness. It is all of the same fabric, almost indistinguishable. In each of these there is value and no value. If the massive mountains are being reclaimed and will be only sand and pebbles, then there is no permanence in this permanence. Yet everything continues, everything is connected.

The closer I stand to beauty and death, connectedness and sorrow, the closer their edges become. I move, rippling from sorrow and fear for my sweet friend Anna to knowing this is the way it is. The leap is terrifying, but then all become equal. My loneliness and lack of a partner are the same as the sweetness of my connection to the earth, to my friends and my community. No longer opposite sides of a paradigm, they are all one continuous piece of fabric. One folds into another, boundaries dissolve, the massiveness and majesty of the earth's canyons are equal to the rubble and sand that flies in your face in a storm. The constant is no constancy. Continuity connects it all.

June 27

We drive back to Salt Lake City and the airport and talk. Traveling with my friend opens me up to a shyness and soft wanting. My life is scraped clean, as if I were a walking skeleton and she a live flesh woman. Her house and garden glow with her touches, mine are subdued and quiet. When she walks, she pauses and looks around. I walk quickly, my goal firmly in sight. There is a grace and ease about her and her life that I admire. I see what I do not have in my life.

My composing life requires me to strip off many of the diversions and comforts of a regular life. These desires are forfeit not out of meanness, but of the necessity of time. My life centers around my work and my daughter, and I cut corners off everything else.

I am an eagle with a strong curved beak, large talons, broad dark wings, looking down with curiosity at the downy thrush or cozy chickadee. I am an older wiry man watching the younger men in a group of cherubic young girls with a frown of envy. I claim responsibility for the life I have chosen; I am lean, austere, vigilant, and many times impatient. My long legs scale my landscape; my eyes are straight ahead. Yet, I mourn the woman I could be, soft, pliant, supportive, enmeshed in a life of things and pleasures—living in the moment. I live in the moment, but not the moment that distracts and sets off in a meandering course like the coils of a beautiful river. My moment connects back to the goal—the work, which is seeing and understanding myself, like a tall, straight tree on the fine trace of a mountain range.

June 30

While I was away, Cassie was nestled in with her cousins for a summer of sailing in Mantoloking. I visit on the weekend, and in August will take my place as den mother. The house continually resounds with high voices, shrieks, and laughter, excitement teeming all around. I sit on my bed with the window and doors open.

I feel quietness inside me. The noise and confusion are difficult for me to handle, yet I feel fractured and broken when I leave to return to Philadelphia for the week. The transition is difficult, and as I drive home, I am both relieved and sad to be by myself.

July 9

The weekend at the shore is quiet. The house is full of children, but I find rest and comfort. I sleep late, hide in my room with work, and come out for disjointed talk.

More heartbreaking news. Tim Pantaleoni, my sister Lâle's old boyfriend, has disappeared. He was living in Oahu and set out to scout a trail in the forest of Maunawili. They found his bike leaning against a fence.

Hawaii is known for its treacherous volcano landscape, old vents covered with jungle foliage. After three days, they called off the official search. After two days they almost never find the lost one.

Lâle flies out to help the family while they continue searching. "He had a hard time," she says over the phone, "letting in the beauty of Hawaii." Is he now absorbed into the beauty? My mind returns to Utah and the cycle of reclamation.

July 10

Monday morning. The magnolia tree is dying by degrees. The slender gray branches cross over each other at the base, this year the leaves are small and pale. Overcast day, foolish thoughts. Where do I place grief?

July 11

I am starting to hear the piece *Over Salt River (Simply for Henry)* dedicated to my cousin Hank; a fabric of glissandos, long and slow, build on oscillating intervals—true circles of motion. Air sounds, linear and snapping, beating of chords. The orchestra imitates the voice with frail nuances, inhalations, and exhalations.

July 18

Wading through incredibly hot and humid weather is like wading in soup. Cassie's room is the only air-conditioned room in the house, and after a few hours in my studio, I am ready to do anything in her room.

The work on the new orchestra piece goes well. I can't quite hear the entire piece, but the melody for the soprano solo comes quickly. I have permission from poet Joy Harjo to use her "Eagle Poem":

> Breathe in, knowing we are made of
> All this, and breathe, knowing
> We are truly blessed because we
> Were born, and die soon within a
> True circle of motion[2]

As I engage, once again the process surprises me. Three weeks ago, I only had an impression of the piece, its general size and weight, as if I were holding an invisible oval shape in my hands. I could only feel the smoothness of the outside shell, the weight in my hands. Gradually, I started to hear the edges, like an egg hissing in a frying pan, the whites gradually crisping under the heat, gaining definition.

The piece, in some way, already exists. Once conceived, the genetic coding is set, the DNA strands are in place; growth occurs as I support and nurture it. There is a certain inevitability, majesty, and grand design, as if I am uncovering a work of art long hidden under decades of dust and dirt. I carefully chip and brush away the debris from an edge, and the whole becomes more revealed. I discover the music as I write it.

July 21

While empathy and compassion are antidotes to judgment and intolerance, these are desperate times for those who wish to alleviate the world's pain through support, education, and opportunity. We are five years from the turn of the century, and the gains of the late '60s and early '70s are being rolled back. Affirmative action is losing ground, educational programs and incentives for the poor and underprivileged are disappearing, and even freedom of speech is threatened.

I keep thinking of Europe as a viable option. I don't know if I am furious and ready to fight, or if this is a time for quiet and relocating to another country. The monk's self-immolation on the streets of Hanoi flashes to mind.

July 23

I try to synthesize my understanding of separation and connection, death and life. What I saw in Utah is only the impetus of transformation. The experience is the catalyst, not the subject. It is the means of the vision, not the vision.

How do I write of death and connection? The last section of the orchestra piece is clear, starting as the still point. Slowly circling, moving up, the last notes breathe into an ecstasy of sound—the kind I love and can hardly bear not to write—swirling, blissful love. But how do I get there? The first two-thirds of the piece are blank. The image of the laundry keeps appearing in my eye, a white dazzling continuous curl of fabric. I hear the wind rushing down the mountains, around my face, in my ears, glancing off my legs, stopping. Then picking up again. The rush of life at its apex, almost a distortion.

Where does pitch begin? Where does rhythm, which is circular, start to spiral up? Must I always write in rhythms, or can I slow the upward turning? What is beauty?

July 31
The last section came leaping out, rippling chords, changing harmonies. Still I am full of doubt. The beginning was difficult. This weekend, I remember to trust the wind, where the piece began.

August 14
The beach is healing. I am calm and working. Cassie and her friends are wonderful, running off to each other's houses or to the beach. Lâle is here, her pale, tense face gleams in the darkness as we talk late on the porch. Tim was not found.

August 21
The past two weeks have not been easy. Having so many little bodies of different ages is overwhelming, as is the noise. But Cassie loves it. She sails on the bay until noon and spends the rest of the day with her friends on the beach. I work on the orchestra piece, but my usual flow is hampered. I am almost ready to plunge in and then I hesitate. Suddenly I am not sure about anything.

September 8
We acclimatize to Philadelphia after a month away. I am glad to be back. I light candles to remind the universe that I am lonely. I ask to be considered.

I have written all the material for *Over Salt River* and begin to put down the first notes. I feel stuporous. Here I am again, like a novice, thrown into the same anxiety and furor of feelings as always. I am skittish, full of adolescent passion, and beside myself. I start with no faith or stamina. I grapple with inertia.

Why is *this* the process for me? I never can remember it, like a mother trying to remember childbirth. I sleep through it, cry through it, suffer it and hold on, knowing that the only way is *through* it. Unless I pierce the uncertainty, it will possess and shape my life.

When I start a new piece, everything sways in the balance. I am a rank beginner; I know nothing and have confidence in nothing. Past experience is meaningless and adult thinking worthless. I am, all at once, a child again, splayed out on the floor, trying to turn over. Fortunately, once I am through the beginning phase, I relax and enjoy it, and rarely do I feel as bare and vulnerable.

September 11

Still feel out of the groove. The fall looms with all the scheduling and conflicts, the running back and forth to the residency in Delaware, balancing Cassie's schedule and my own—it is more than I anticipated. I am torn when I leave Cassie in aftercare or take her to late evening rehearsals. The planning is exhausting.

October 14

I have a fleeting fantasy, a secret fear; I will turn into music, just this vehicle for sound. Music will overtake me, fill my pores, and submerge me. I will wake up one morning scaled and encrusted like an ancient desert creature, a reptile with congealed flesh. A watcher.

October 15

What responsibility do I have to the political in my music? In the recent year, I have developed an attitude of speaking out as an artist. Partly because of my national residency and partly because artists often fail to articulate their contributions to the world.

I am uncomfortable with the elitism we have spawned for ourselves as artists. We congratulate ourselves with the "you are so talented" and "how do you ever do that" image the public has of us. The adoration isolates me and rarefies the art form. Artists are indeed talented, and what they do is many times amazing. But only in the context that life is amazing and miraculous, only as it connects and does not separate us from life.

I speak about my work and my understanding as much as possible. Stepping out, I name myself as an artist. When I share, both in person and in the work, I break and chip pieces off the monolith of elitism that separates us from others.

Committed visibility. I turn this over in my mind.

November 8

Over Salt River is complete. It was both difficult and easy. The first six minutes were hard to write, without any particular reason, but the rest flowed easily. I will let the piece rest before the final corrections and copying.

November 9

Anna is again sick. Another tumor, and now chemotherapy. Can I bear this?

November 10

Soon I start to work on a string sextet, a commission from Wilmington Music Festival. The work celebrates the hundredth anniversary of Brahms' death. I love his sextets. He opens the door from the very first note, and you delight in sound, energy, and harmony. There is no subtext; all is swirls and moves with color, alive and real. I cannot write in imitation of Brahms, nor will I use any of his melodies in my piece; but like him, I want to be there, right in the first moment, in the flow and radiance.

November 28

I hear snatches of the new piece, *It Is My Heart Singing*. The opening is widening circles of the sound, whirling, an ecstasy of the galaxies. The word *dervish* means doorway, an open space through which something can happen. "I just reached that part of myself that's invisible," says Rumi.

Rumi, Rilke, and Whitman are poets of ecstasy, and beyond words. I just find myself nodding and smiling as I read.

November 29

I napped yesterday, dreaming about the piece. I fell into a deep sleep and unsettling dream.

There is a black thread down my throat. The end is down my esophagus. I realize it is Cassie's thread from her sewing project, and a needle is attached to it. I find a broken needle lodged into the back of my throat. I pull it out.

Out of my throat comes this piece.

December 30
A clear birthday morning, my forty-third year. The days go fast, and I tumble out of bed into this new piece. I leave my composing desk each afternoon with a measure of wondering and calm. The work is all about arrivals and being in a place I do not know, except in dreams. I gain entrance by turning. Faster and faster I twist in my music, until the energy is no longer earthbound. It shoots up, glowing and iridescent. The blooming of the heart, pulling off delicate outer layers, deeper and deeper into the soul.

Chapter 21

MANY ARE CALLED

Across the brown-green Schuylkill River, streets are shaded by tall trees, with large Victorian duplexes rising above walkways. Spring brings the weeping cherry trees to bloom; petals fall like snow; magnolias burst and die with the frost. Trash is piled high on the curb and noise is continual. Cars rush by screaming their radios, and over by the trolley portal, the one-car subway screeches on its tracks. The humid air of the tunnel brushes my face as I plunge downtown, a welcome relief from the smell of urine.

Philadelphia in the late '70s is dirty and crime ridden. Frank Rizzo is in the middle of his tenure; racial strife and police brutality are endemic. MOVE explodes in Powelton Village, with another conflict ten years later that burns sixty-five houses to the ground.

But under the grime and tension is a diversity and energy I love. Streets are crowded with a burst of lunchtime colors and swirling skirts, crisp suits and ties jostle me as I walk. A baby cries from a stroller, shushed by a teen, her hair piled high in braids, a panhandler sits on the corner with a dirty dog. Smells assault and lure me on, I follow the hum, the underground burble. I call this city mine.

~⚬~

I moved to Philadelphia after graduating from Bennington College in the summer of 1976. I wanted to get to know my father, Britton Chance, better. I planned to stay for a year or two and then move to New York City where my real musical life would begin.

He offered me a job helping him around the lab at the University of Pennsylvania. "How about $6,000 a year for a salary?" he proposed. My eyes widened; that seemed like a lot of money to me. "I'll throw in an extra $500 for taxes," he generously added. I quickly rented a studio apartment on Pine Street, a large room with a tiny kitchen, sparsely furnished with borrowed furniture—a bed, chair, and dresser. I was astonished to find that rent was more than a third of my salary.

I composed in the mornings and arrived at work after lunch at the famous Richards Building designed by architect Louis Kahn. Tall and austere, the laboratories were housed in three towers attached to a fourth tower, with one large central room for scientists to gather and exchange ideas—perfect for my father's style of collaborative work. His office was always noisy. He sat at his large high desk ringed with stools, looking at data. Scientists and postdoctoral fellows trying to catch his attention slipped in and around the stools like trout. A phone call—mid-sentence he'd swivel his chair to take it, then turn back and finish his thought.

I did whatever was needed. Sitting in the tiny office outside his room with his office manager, I filed, ordered supplies, or ran errands. The secretary sitting at the desk in the hallway answered the phones and pounded on the large Smith Corona electric typewriter, typing and retyping his scientific papers. Later, I would learn to do the accounting for all the many research grants. And finally, I took over the drafting shop, creating charts, graphs, and drawings for the scientists' publications and grant applications. I loved keeping the testy Rapidograph pens clean, cutting fresh sheets of velum from the roll, and lettering with an old engineering template; it held me safe against the surrounding chaos.

At the end of the workday, I was often invited to dinner. I trotted after my father's bike as he talked in his gravelly voice, pausing now and then to let me catch up. Later, I trotted back to the lab with him for another two hours of work before going home.

All the time I was composing and trying to figure out how to go about my musical life. My parents wanted me to go to graduate school. My brilliant and renegade Bennington teacher Henry Brant, however, had no time for graduate school. "Just write music!" he practically shouted. "Write for your friends. Get it performed. Write more."

Working full-time, I was allowed to take two courses a semester at the University of Pennsylvania for free. I enthusiastically learned how to play a sitar, blundered through a harmony class, and finally wrangled a graduate composition class with a well-known composer. One fall afternoon, I brought in the first piece I had written after college for review, a large piece for a full band that I had labored over. I glowed with pride and exhaustion.

The eminent composer gravely considered my composition. We sat quietly, expectantly, in chairs scattered around the graduate seminar room. Slowly, he turned the pages. The crisp sheets crackled. He looked without comment, and finally closed the score. Sitting back, he crossed his legs and lit a cigarette. Smoke floated and swirled around his face. "Many are called, but few are chosen," he finally said.

We were silent; the criticism was implicit. I froze, but my brain whirled frantically. "Get out of here!" it screamed. "Get away from teachers like this!"

That spring I went to a concert of new music by the Relâche Ensemble at the Painted Bride Art Center. The converted bridal shop was narrow, and we were packed together on hard wooden folding chairs. The air was hot and almost unbreathable; we fanned ourselves with the programs. The soprano stepped into the light and began performing Berio's *Sequenza*. Wildly dressed and made up like an Egyptian queen, Barbara Noska's dark, sensuous voice held me.

There were few music groups in Philadelphia at that time and none who were as dedicated to performing current contemporary music as Relâche. Founded by composer Joseph Franklin and conductor and trombonist Joe Showalter, the ensemble was a collective run by local composers. Soon I joined as a composer, performer, and administrator of the ensemble.

I composed continually for Barbara and the ensemble. I experimented with extended vocal techniques and adapted to the odd, fluctuating instrumental combination of the Relâche by creating works for unspecified instrumentation. We performed mostly experimental music—music on the fringe—and my vocabulary grew steadily with the continual exposure to Earl Brown, Morton Feldman, Robert Ashley, Alvin Lucier, Terry Riley, and of course, the wonderful Pauline Oliveros.

What began as a year's adventure in Philadelphia turned into much more. I moved to an apartment in a cheaper, poorer neighborhood. The first night there were gunshots, and the car outside my building had its windshield shattered. The son of the downstairs tenant punched a hole through the wall into the common hallway, and the roaches were so big that I would stand on the bed at night and peer into the hallway to make sure all was in the clear. But the space was large and sunny. I painted it a garish apricot. My piano, too big to be brought up the stairs, sat a few blocks away in a small room in a building owned by my stepmother. There I practiced and composed for hours, leaving with the smell of mildew on my clothing.

I was busy with several jobs: my work at the lab, Relâche, performing on the piano, and an occasional small commission. Every time I got a raise, however, I reduced my hours a bit to make more time for my music. I fantasized about giving myself a sabbatical, a time dedicated solely to my work, and began saving $1,000 a year. Twelve years later, a large commission under my belt, I quit my jobs and hurled myself into full-time work as a composer. I was to stay in Philadelphia for twenty-five years.

"Many are called, but few are chosen,"[1] says Jesus at the end of the parable of the wedding feast. What does he mean? The word *chosen* implies a selection process. Jesus smiles; he is too full of love for exclusion. Well-known psychiatrist and best-selling author Scott Peck deciphers it for me. "All of us are called by and to grace," he writes, "but few of us choose to listen to the call."[2]

We are called; we do not listen. We have the capacity; we get sidetracked, scared, angry, or confused. Scarcity is a false god. The world is large and full. The ability to create is a birthright. To be chosen, then, is merely to respond to the invitation. We only need to believe and surround ourselves with those who say a resounding, infinite yes.

Chapter 22

SPIRIT

Philadelphia (1996)

I had really connected to the ancient knowledge that we all have, and that is it was really a matter not of trying to learn something, but of remembering.

Alice Walker[1]

January 2

A newness is in the air. I point to the only direction visible: to create, as Alice Walker writes, out of the "ancient knowledge." I cannot learn or study this, only remember what I have always known—that of the divine. I smell it in the wind, and I feel it when I plunge my hands in the spring earth.

Yet I am caught, snagged on the word. I can't move forward. In my suffering-coded world, the divine is the *end* of the journey. Once the destination is reached, life is over. Moreover, suffering and pain are complex, joy and love are simple and unworthy of an artist's palette.

But this cannot be. I am foolish. Do I believe that love, beauty, spaciousness, and blessedness are less complex, less rich than pain and suffering? (Secretly I do.)

I desire a life without missing, without longing or incompleteness. If I commit to living as if *this* day is enough, then I am complete and blessed. The divine is right now, without additions or waiting, just this most delicious moment. I transform from lack to fullness, from loneliness to unity, and from darkness to light. Yet I hesitate.

Tell me the difference between imagining and remembering.

January 5
Carolyn Forché's poetry is shattering. Her work is a fulcrum through which the suffering of the world is seen and acknowledged. In her simple, evocative verse, she witnesses the torture victims of Central America. She carefully skirts the dark side of suffering that is glamorous and intense—suffering as being. In this distortion, pain gives life form and substance. Forché is the vehicle for others and stands clear.

I wonder if I give my darkness too much substance. But how can I give it up?

January 8
Snow has been raging for days now. Over twenty-five inches and still snowing. The streets are shrouded, houses and cars covered. The house reflects the grayness of sky. We are home. I sit quietly with myself. A hibernation, a resting place to consider.

January 18
I have returned from several days of editing the recording of the new release of my works for CRI, Emergency Music. Outside my window is early morning fog and drizzle. The warmth melts the snow slowly. I feel the sweetness of being with my music today. The intensity is clearly focused. My new maxim is to be curious and not anxious.

February 2

I dream of houses. A portent of change, these dreams come when I am reassessing my soul. I hold a long, thin baby snake in my hand; the tail is broken off. We go up to the second floor, through a narrow hallway. I step into an immense auditorium. The rows of seats descend to a stage filled with students laughing and clapping. I sit next to a man. The dance is in honor of his work over the many years. His wife is large, and she dances for him; her naked breasts are round and beautiful.

February 3

I resist. I know where I must go into a life that includes the spirit, yet I have been scratching at my perceptions. I block myself from being clear, open, and on task. It is more efficient to be short and irritable, and momentarily satisfying. And there is something about my darkness that is embarrassing to admit—its addictive deliciousness. I feel a secret ennoblement, a heroic pleasure.

I disappoint myself.

The new dwelling revealed in my dream waits. My bags are packed, all is ready. Ten years of soul work and suddenly I want to be short, abrupt, and say what is on my mind without prejudice. Empathy winks at me, lurking. Open to another's pain, I am vulnerable. Judgment flies up to protect me. Who will protect me without these judgments? How will I connect without a constant empathetic bleeding?

February 15

McMichael Elementary School is in the Mantua neighborhood of Philadelphia. I park and walk to the front door, waiting to be buzzed in. Plastic bags whirl in the wind as if they were tumbleweed. Vacant lots between row houses are covered in trash. But once inside, the warm, eager faces of my Young Composers embrace me.

Timothy stands close to me. When I move, he moves. He waits for me to play his piece with him and follows me like a shadow around the room. I help Shante with her instrument, calm Ferron down so he can concentrate, and get sidelined by Brandi and Terrell. They work on a piece for two desks and their hands. Experimenting with fingers, palms, and fists, they make sounds on the wooden tops. I step back and almost fall over Timothy; he is patient. Jake and Michael struggle with their invented notation. Jake's face contorts; he cannot figure out how to write his rhythm down. We put words to the melody, and suddenly he claps it with ease.

Timothy pushes me toward the piano and I grab a drum. His piece is carefully notated in tiny print. Only he knows what it means, but he has taught me. He begins to play, his long fingers curving around the complicated chords. A dreamy look comes over his face. "How will I know when to stop?" I press him. He continues to play, immersed in his own sound world.

February 24

The work on *It Is My Heart Singing* is going well, particularly the first four minutes. As I edge into the rhythmic section, I realize I need to expand my vision of rhythm. Rethinking the whole concept, I reinvent myself. Where does the energy start, this ripple of life?

The premiere of *Since Singing Is Being* disappoints. The work was poorly rehearsed and had some murky writing. It was a transition piece; it could have been better.

February 26
Anna Cholakian died today in the early morning, seven months after the neck cancer diagnosis. She was thirty-three. We are full of sorrow. I am in my studio every day; the string sextet is almost finished. The writing is more complex than usual and full of long melodies and soaring harmonies. Anna fills me while I write.

April 1
My heart is opening in strange ways. Jasmine is one of the smallest students in my Young Composer class. I am fascinated with her face, her sculpted skin, her beautifully defined chin. I love her intelligence, quickness, and glow. She sits before a drum set she has made out of two oatmeal cans, delicately separated by a purple hair roller. "Listen to this," she says as she taps out a rhythm. "And this one." She wants to hold my attention. Later, she writes an elaborate piece, using a red marker on newsprint. She tries to get her group to rehearse the piece, but they fall to the floor in giggles. Jasmine angrily hits one of them on the head and is sent out of the classroom.

She is usually not there when I come to teach; she is either sick or in detention. I miss her. One day she is back and sits in the corner of the room with her drums. "That one," I say to her teacher, pointing to Jasmine. "I'd take her home in a minute." Her bland face doesn't change. "That would be a terrible mistake; she's trouble," she says flatly. Then a rare smile. "But her grandmother would be delighted."

April 6
I start working on the opera *Billy and Zelda* with seriousness. At least with the characteristic procrastination that seriousness demands.

In the recent weeks, full of Anna's memorial, my thoughts are with dead children. Billy and Zelda, the two main characters in my opera, and their desires to be held and quieted. Billy, killed in the war, returns so that he can finally be free of his mother's grief, which haunts him and keeps him immobile. Zelda, the angry waif child who died in childhood, returns to be called in and found. The overlay is my own lost child. I wrestle to stand clear and tell their stories cleanly. Without falling into my own.

April 15

"What is composing music all about?" I asked the class. I am teaching another Young Composer session, this time to sixth graders. I scribble their thoughts about music quickly on the blackboard: writing your own tune, expressing yourself, giving the beat, listening to yourself, being famous, making money. I wipe the chalk from my hands. "Creating your own song, being heard, witnessing," I suggest. They stop for a moment. "Creating yourself." They are quiet.

Music has this element of bearing witness; it is that space where I reveal all that I am and dream of who I am becoming. I noticed it most distinctly when I worked with the homeless women, helping them to write operas about their lives. It was slow and oftentimes painful work as they told their stories and wrote lyrics and songs. But it was there that I truly saw the raw power of art for the first time—the ability to transform, to reach beyond the "dailyness" of living to the reinvention of self. To sing about oneself is to be visible. To witness life is to stand apart and speak one's truth. To perform a work together is to collaborate for clarity of the moment.

April 16
The morning is dark and warm, a steamy moisture; a mourning dove cries its haunting call. I am on the brink of learning something about myself. I wait.

May 4
The trillium begin to close and the sweet smell of wisteria pervades the air. Fading crab apple blossoms cover the walk. I sit and read.

Rumi waited for his beloved, Shams-i Tabriz, who came and went, came again, and finally disappeared forever. "Why should I seek?" Rumi asks. "I am the same as he/His essence speaks through me. I have been looking for myself."[2]

Always the search for the other, the cosmic yearning, and finding it where I am.

May 15
My Young Composers are writing their own composition and preparing to perform for their school friends, teachers, and parents. Because music-making is a group activity, I teach them how to work together as a team, to stay focused and attentive during the performance, and to follow the directions of the conductor. They take turns conducting each other in large group works.

Sasha and Jade are the most difficult to engage in this class. They are best friends in the worst sense. They sit together, whispering to each other or literally falling asleep at their desks. I have to wake Jade on a regular basis. Over the course of the residency, they grudgingly pretend to write a composition together. Hoping to encourage them, I ask them to come to the front of the class and play their piece for the other students. They slowly slouch forward, bumping into each other, and fuss with the music. I wonder why I am bothering. Why don't I ignore them altogether? But I persist.

I find I teach as much about performance as I do composition. The act of performance is complex and is a metaphor for being visible. It takes poise and maturity. These sixth graders, on the cusp of adolescence, are, frankly, a mess. They slump. They begin playing suddenly when everyone is talking. They grab their music and march off the stage before the last note is played. They burst into giggles at any hint of a mistake. I work patiently with each set of composers-now-performers, reminding them how to show respect for themselves, their creation, and their audience.

Sasha and Jade are no exception. As they perform for the class they have several false starts. They get halfway through the piece and grind to a halt. I drill them again and again. There is a lot of smirking as they move back to their seats. They are not going to give me an inch.

The pair drives me to distraction, but somehow, miraculously, they finish a piece called *Dance of Creation*. During the performance they hold themselves a little bit straighter than I have ever seen them. I hold my breath, but they are fine. They perform their piece and it is all theirs. As the applause sweeps over them, they stand there accepting the hard-won praise. Sasha's lip curls and Jade's face shines. They suddenly recognize their accomplishment, and I am so proud of them.

June 5

Over Salt River and *It Is My Heart Singing* had great performances. The Newark Symphony had the audience both in tears and on their feet. The string sextet was fluid and soaring. One melody followed after another. The new musical turn excites me. I am eager to continue working in that direction for the upcoming commission.

The work on the opera *Billy and Zelda* is constant and good. The director, Ben Levit, and I spend hours each week together, working on the script. Invaluable is his ability to listen intently and ask good questions. I have written eight songs of the fifteen needed for the workshop.

July 21

I pick up Cassie at camp. Last year she was the long-legged Bambi, weeping when I left and delighted when I returned. This summer she is filled with dark looks and silences. "Oh! I just can't explain," she broods. "Don't touch me!" when in public.

August 10

Last night, the full moon shone. The pull to the spiritual has been strong, seeping into my friendships and work. All of what I do is somehow spiritual; I have been afraid to name it. I am surprised others see it in me, or that it manifests naturally.

So what is all this? The universe offers me a clarification and deepening of my spiritual nature. Perhaps it is the work of the next decade, as my physical and emotional well-being was the work of the last decade. Should I submit to this? It will take me on a wild path, one that I can chart only as I experience it. The hand is outstretched. I fear what I must give up. I ask the moon on its full night that I learn to be fully as I am—whatever that state is—and that I submit and surrender.

October 12

"When you sing," says Saint Augustine, "you pray twice." Crickets chirp with candor and cars swoosh by. Sound is sacred in all its manifestations. The voice comes out of the dark, dank breath, truth warmed by my core. My vision is that we all find ourselves as the music and song.

October 13

Prayer. I have not prayed since I was a child. Joy Harjo reminds me, "To pray, you open your whole self up."[3]

When I dance, I pray. I open from my heart line. Moving close to the ground, I jump up and circle my hands above my head. The whirling dervishes turn round and round and find their way to the God, to the divine, to the light.

I am uncomfortable using the word God. The predominant definition is spare and somewhat mean. The male characterization makes him difficult to consider. Yet I cannot deny a spiritual, powerful force in my life.

October 16

This has been a month of struggle and adjustment. Cassie grapples with middle school, and I am exhausted from the writing schedule of the opera. My cupboards are bare. *Billy and Zelda* continues to stir up the losses I had as a child. Working with both sisters, Eva and Lâle, to create the script and lyrics is an added upheaval.

But always, the bridge from the old world to the new one is love. The pregnant neighbor extends her love to Billy and his mother. The narrator finds Zelda and brings the errant ghost home. Love offers the path into the new world, on whose edge I stand.

October 21

The morning is gray against the sounds of cars passing on Baltimore Avenue, and the floors in my studio pop with the change in temperature. I listen to the new thing growing inside and outside of me.

This begins a different kind of living. My body and heart are changing but my mind lags behind. Adolescent soft bumps and curves develop in reverse.

November 19

Spirituality is an act of being. I stand at the center and live as it widens around me. I am connected to the hum of the earth, the breath of my daughter. It is not looking for the answer; it is merely the connection. Anytime I stop and listen, I am in the spirit.

Going home.

Chapter 23

OLYMPIC BABY

Early fall and the evenings are already starting to cool. After a long day of graduate classes, she arrives for the night shift to type his many grant proposals and scientific papers. Her tea-length skirt is cinched snug at the waist, her fitted top is covered by a flared coat with large buttons. Maybe she is wearing her brown peep-toe heels, or even a hat.

He sits at his desk in the darkened laboratory, his work illuminated by a lamp. He looks up as she enters, and smiles. She is slender, bright, and soft. He is worldly, debonair, charismatic, and terribly attractive.

A piece of paper slips off the lab table. They both reach for it and bump heads. That moment starts their seven-year relationship. She does not ask if he is married, and he doesn't mention it.

❧

My father, George Britton Chance, was born into a family of inventors and engineers. He quickly discarded his first name and became Brit to his friends, BC to his colleagues, and D to his family.

273

He had a passion for sailing and an uncanny knack for creating simple solutions for complex problems. He invented an automatic steering device as a teenager, the stopped-flow spectrometer (now a standard research instrument) during his graduate work, and was part of a secret team that developed the radar during WWII. Later, he became the director of the Johnson Research Foundation at the University of Pennsylvania, and over the next thirty years, turned it into an international center. And from start to finish he sailed, winning a gold medal at the 1952 Helsinki Summer Olympics in 5.5 meter racing the year I was born; I was his "Olympic" baby.

The Olympic trials were in the spring of 1951. He returned flushed with the success of getting on the sailing team; my mother got pregnant. They made plans that she would travel to Sweden, a country that was open to unwed mothers. She would give birth to me and return after his divorce. She did not tell anyone, not her mother or her sister or her best friend, Dorothy. I was born during the coldest, darkest time in Sweden, almost on the last day of the year.

Their love story did not end well. After having placed me with Solvig, she returned to Philadelphia. He was still married. Refusing to see him, she completed her PhD degree and found a job in Athens, Ohio. They reconciled as his divorce was being finalized and decided to marry. She would, however, first go to Sweden as a guest lecturer and return with me the following year. They wrote each other every day.

My mother was gone only a few months when my father met a beautiful society woman, a widower with four young children. He stopped writing. Perhaps bringing his lover and their illegitimate child home was too much for him. Perhaps the custody battle with his first wife left him wanting to unite his children with another big family. He broke off his engagement with my mother and married Lil.

I was not quite six months when my mother placed me in a foster home at the southern tip of Sweden. I was three and half when I saw her next. Heartbroken. Jilted.

What can I make of all this? And how do I explain with an understanding to his faults? He was ambitious, shrewd, brilliant, and often unkind. He loved women, had three wives and many, many girlfriends. "Don't sing love songs," sings Joan Baez in her ballad. "My father was a handsome devil/ He had a chain ten thousand miles long/ And on every link a heart would dangle."

As many times as he was unfaithful to his wives, as many children as he had outside his marriages, he kept in touch with his many lovers, supporting them faithfully with phone calls, letters, and encouragement over the years. He was attracted to smart, career-oriented women and helped them long after the passion died out. He was a difficult, short-tempered father, yet he loved his eleven children, including those of us born out of wedlock.

I was a teenager when I first met my father, a distinguished-looking-man with graying hair. Over the years, we were able to experience our relatedness without childhood damage to tarnish its worth. Our likeness appeared in startling ways: the ability to focus and work in the midst of confusion, a bawdy sense of humor, a love of dark chocolate, and the way the tip of our tongue reaches out for food. But primarily, our commonality was in the abiding passion for the work we love.

He was the only one of my parents who saw *me*, saw the creative in me and saw it as kindred. Unlike my mother, who liked to bask in the romantic notion of me being a composer, he saw the directness of the daily process. He nurtured me with stray comments. Never effusive or wordy, his quiet confidence in me bolstered mine. It was in the ease of the questions, the "How is your work doing today?" followed by a reassuring smile, a pat on my hand.

He showed me the soul of an artist—an individual who has total focus on a passion, and who knows that this is the life he or she must lead, no matter what and how long. It is oftentimes lonely, with long periods of solitude. Flashes of joy and excitement are followed by sudden deflation of disappointment. The difficulty, I find, is in maintaining the balance between the everyday and the work; it consumes most of my waking moments, distracts me from my family, and even haunts my sleep.

Over the years I watched him go to his lab every day, reviewing grants, writing papers, discussing data with colleagues, generously sharing thoughts and ideas. No matter how late in the day or how late in his life, he worked continuously, carefully, with the grace of a long-distance runner. When I became confused at my purpose, I'd recall how he kept going, did the work no matter what, and continued when all others have stopped or retired. There was utter simplicity in this connection: I am at work, I am the work; a flow in and out.

Chapter 24

TURNING

Philadelphia (1997)

Daylight, full of small dancing particles
and the one great turning, our souls
are dancing with you, without feet, they dance.
Can you see them when I whisper in your ear?

Rumi[1]

March 25

The two-week opera workshop for *Billy and Zelda* was a whole cascade of words, from wonderful to terrible, frightening to reassuring, painful to intensely gratifying—all that is both contradictory and intense. The work is fine. Zelda flashes with theater and improvised sound. Billy, solidly flesh and blood, is expressive and beautiful. The cast was terrific and the music director, Alan Johnson, a true musician. Ben Levit staged the work exquisitely.

I have not written songs like this before. First I read Eva's lyrics for days, and then a slight melody or rhythmic sensibility occurs to me. Quickly, the material tumbles out, and the whole song is there. Sometimes it is like birthing an egg. There is the brief waiting, a quick straining, a distortion of my face, and, like magic, the song slips out like a glistening, warm orb. I wrote over twelve songs in three months.

March 29

Nights are filled with dreams. After an intense day of work, I wake several times a night hearing my music, or watching it slowly, scrutinizing every moment. My mind is like a computer I am forced to watch, slowly processing every twist and turn. Privacy is invaded. Even when I sleep the music wakes me up, possesses me. I roll over in bed. "Get back to the studio where you belong," I mutter. But other times, I am fascinated and observe my mind function on a most basic level. One night I watched the entire opera pass before me as if under a microscope. The ends and next beginnings of each song were meticulous. Then my dreams turn threatening. They are invaded by murderers who want to kill me. I wake hot and sweaty.

March 30

"Now I can tell you this" is one of Eva's lyrics from the opera. My understanding of opera and song has deepened since I began to write.

Opera, in its classical form, is a continuous singing from beginning to end. Always shunning its more popular sibling, music theater or musical, it has no dialog. Instead the narration is held in the recitative, or *recitativo*, sung-speech that tells the action of story.

I have grown to hate the sound of recitative and often call it wretched-ative. Contemporary opera librettos are littered with the inconsequential—a knock, an opening of a window—bathed in a swatch of sound that has no direction, cloaked as recitative. Ben, my director, has taught me well: "show me, don't tell me" is often more than enough.

Singing, particularly in opera, has a sacredness about it; emerging from the depths of my body, it is a moment when I utter my most intimate thoughts. Truth-telling—a moment of revelation, insight, or growth—is where I am right now. And always in the beauty of words, a rich variety of poetic words. As I compose, I taste each word, like a small, beautiful stone. I pour through each line, looking for meaning. Listen to the lyrics of the final song of the opera that Eva created:

Like the core of the earth
Traveling at a different speed
From its surface, so this baby's heart
Travels against mine, faster, smaller,
Working hard against the rhythm.

I'd do anything
to scour the name off its brow
to call it my own, but
It's been called into the world,
To go its own orbit like the moon.

Who can say
This was not meant to be,
Somehow, somewhere, this precious person
Singing forth its own song.[2]

April 1

Is *Billy and Zelda* the only opera whose main character is pregnant, and whose subject is the greatest love story of all—that with our children?

April 21
The warmth of spring unearths an old melancholy. Nothing is enough, even after the wonderful opera workshop and a performance at Carnegie Hall of *They Come Dancing*. My process is full of doubts and fears that press through in weak moments.

I stay at home with Cassie, play in the garden, and help her pack for her trip.

April 30
My three-year residency in Delaware is winding down. We sit in meetings and talk about outcomes or measurable results of my work in the community setting. Do my students get better grades? Are the homeless women more successful after working with me? Or, at the very least, have we created new audiences for the arts? These are reasonable questions. If one puts in the effort and money, shouldn't there be a tangible, visible result? I shake my head. It is really none of my business.

I teach because I believe in the power of creativity is in all of us, just unrecognized. I teach because I trust it will take root in some strange and unimagined way, in its own time. I teach as an act of faith, a spiritual practice. I get up every day and do it. "Here," I say, "this is what I have for you today."

I find no master strokes or large, efficient gestures. Only this one-on-one, slow work that brings others into a meaningful connection to the arts—hopefully. A commitment to work close to the ground.

May 17
I start to feel rested and eager to work again. I travel to Minneapolis to work with the Greater Twin Cities Youth Orchestra—all nine

280

of them. The premiere of *StarFire* will be done by their elementary school players. They delight me with the seriousness of their playing and their ardent questions. I love the contrast of writing for young performers; it is in perfect balance with works for professional orchestras and ensembles.

June 9

Summer begins. I am a composer-in-residence at the Seal Bay Festival for two weeks. Twelve miles off the coast of Maine, Vinalhaven is an island of smooth granite beaches and bright blue seas. Seal mothers and their pups bask on the rocks at sunset.

Along with other composers and the Cassatt String Quartet, I reside at composer Dan Godfrey's family homes out on the peninsula, surrounded by the Penobscot Bay. The festival is a much-needed break from the struggle of uncertainties and the everyday details. I have not been overly graceful.

The issue of spirituality in my work and life continues to speak to me. I desire it and am uninterested at the same time. I know where I must go, but resist. Why am I pulled forward with heels dug in?

June 11

The magic of the beautiful island works on me. I make revisions to the opera, slowly wondering about the orchestration. Eva gave birth to a second son today. We talk on the phone. She is soft and full of wonder.

June 14

It has been delightful to get to know iconic Joan Towers, one of the other resident composers. She has great charm and warmth.

Listening to her music, I sense a connection to the earth and sky. Her work is muscular in an interesting way, with moments of tenderness; there is always a sense of balance and elasticity.

I have revised *It Is My Heart Singing* for piano and string quartet and work with the wonderful Cassatt Quartet daily, getting ready for the performance.

June 18

I do not sleep well. I am stupid and gawky. I am confused and dumb. What change of chemistry, creeping dissatisfaction has come on me? I am painfully human and adolescent. In the morning I search my face for signs of aging.

June 20

The sunrise wakes me early. I sit out on the large white boulders near the bay and eat an orange. The sun glimmers on the water, and the slices lie succulent and dewy on the plate. A large ant crawls up my pant leg onto the plate. He daintily walks the margin on the inner circle of porcelain, and finally comes to a small drop of orange juice. For a long moment he waits, then flattening himself, legs bent, he drinks.

The supplicant. Open to the nectar of life.

July 12

Spirituality, for me, was always "filled with spirit" or filled with the "other." Never found in religion, old women did it, the witches of Endor. They brimmed with passion, fervor, with the unnamable other.

July 15

I return from Seal Bay and spend a weekend with women friends. I am reminded what I easily forget: my birthright is connection to the divine.

Why do I keep losing track of the heartbeat? The new path is easily lost. What I knew long ago, I rediscover again and again.

August 1

Ecstasy: to stand outside oneself. "Man is concerned with man and forgets the whole and the flowing."[3]

August 30

I hold two beliefs about love, one conscious, the other secret. My adult self wants companionship that supports my work, my family, and gives me a balance of privacy. My secret self wants to be cleansed of the hurt and pain, the long loneliness I have borne since Sweden. He will love me. She will come and wash me clean. He will fill all my cracks and bumps. She will clasp me in her arms. I will be whole, shiny, new, and oh so clean and fresh.

My secret belief hurts me. I have, already, so much love: friends, family, my beloved daughter. I diminish the love I have with the love I desire.

November 15

This period has been difficult and long—a sense of vertigo, unsureness, knowing where I must go, and balking. Can I leave the grief behind and plunge ahead? Then I remember to be more coherent: step into the joy, accept the great other. There is no giving up, only opening up.

This is the way it should be—obscure and clear as a bell. Always complex but with intent to learn what is before me. I am in the exact spot I need to be, regardless of doubling back and confusion.

"To turn, turn will be our delight," say the Shakers, "till by turning, turning we come 'round right." A path rediscovered is a joyous path indeed.

December 15

My music is always my guide. The long rhythmic passages I write in most of my pieces are a marathon run of the soul, the process of surrendering to the larger unnamable whole.

At first I run light-footed, and the rhythms are enthusiastic and playful. My intellect enjoys the gait, the wind, and the smell of the earth. I begin to tire a bit, and I am absorbed in the pounding of my soles on the ground, the intricacies and overlaps. But soon my mind weakens to the muscular fatigue, and the rhythms swell.

Now there is no energy left; I can go no further. As I start to fall, there is a moment of pure supplication; my heart leaves my body and lifts upward to the color and sound that is beyond words. There is no hesitation, no intellectual chatter, just a slow, graceful fall upward.

December 24

Christmas Eve. The children are almost in bed, gathering Santa's midnight snack. Cassie looks pale and clear. I sit by the fire in my sister's living room; the spruce tree sparkles with white lights. Eva wraps gifts upstairs. The paper crunches and crinkles.

What is my Christmas wish? Let me be open to the love and connection I already have and let me gently separate loneliness from my image of love. Let love soar.

I lie back on the rug. The fire heats my face. What would it be like to be in a state of continual joy, in the delight of the moment? I hear a new piece for string quartet. It whispers in my ear.

Celestial beings, they say, reflect the glory of God in word and song, worshipping ceaselessly. They are absorbed in the contemplation of the divine; the seraphim chant Hebrew prayers endlessly in the vibrations of love. They dance and rejoice with the whole being.

The delight of angels.

Chapter 25

FORGIFENESSE

In my dream, I endlessly drag a body in a sack around the dirt-floored basement of my Philadelphia home. Around my arms and across my back, a thin twine is harnessed to my shoulder. I pull the long sack, my muscles stretching painfully. I am exhausted, but still I tug back and forth. The basement air, moist and oppressive, is edged with heating oil and coal dust.

I wake to a clear morning in the early fall. Light fills the room; chrysanthemums have not quite bloomed. The twisted crab apple sighs and sways. A word is in my mouth: forgiveness.

❧

From the Middle English, *forgifenesse*, Old English *forgifennys*, forgiveness is defined as "to grant free pardon and to give up all claim on account of an offense or debt." It is an ongoing process that is not easily accomplished. Peter asked Jesus, "Lord, how many times shall I forgive my brother when he sins against me? Up to seven times?" Jesus answered (smiling, I am sure), "I tell you, not seven times, but seventy-seven times."[1]

Clarissa Pinkola Estes speaks of forgiveness as a great act of creation. There are four stages. The first is to forgo, let it go from memory. The second is to forebear, abstain from punishing. The third is to forget, refuse to dwell upon. The final stage is to forgive—to abandon the debt—give up, withdraw, drop, or jettison the offense. Forgiveness does not sacrifice protection, instead removes the coldness, the death of what lies just behind the rage. "You are not waiting for anything," she tells us. "You are free to go." [2]

When Cassie was six, we adopted a sandy brown American Staffordshire Bull Terrier with a soft black muzzle and delicate ears. That winter I had become obsessed with owning a dog. My husband and I looked at several dogs. When Sophie came bounding out, skidding on the wooden floor and flopping down on her back, we were both smitten. Less than a year later, my husband and I separated. I was grateful for her company and protection.

Sophie was a lovely, lanky, muscle-bound dog with a lethal mouth. She was our constant companion and beloved by my daughter. Sophie took her job in the house seriously and investigated every sound with focus. Outside she was a liability. She shot after squirrels and treed raccoon babies. Once she whipped a mother opossum in the air, showering us with hairless babies. To my utter mortification, she provoked numerous dog fights, butting other dogs with her chest and standing at attention on her short legs. When she ran, she lowered her head with the seriousness of a bull. But nothing was personal; she wasn't mean. She lived with dedication and joy, running back to me with white foam on her lips, a delighted prance in her step.

I walked Sophie twice a day through the streets of Philadelphia. We lived on a beautiful old block of Victorian duplexes, the high stone facades, ten-foot shuttered windows, and iron wrought fences. Sophie and I crossed over Baltimore Avenue, where the trolleys run screeching into the underground tunnel, and walked west.

I often thought about my family as I walked. My relationship with my mother was in tatters. Therapy had opened my Pandora's box and I reached out to her for information about Sweden. The more I asked, however, the more self-protective she became. She accused me of misremembering the past, prying into business that was not mine, and of putting myself, selfishly, before her privacy and safety. When I began planning my wedding, she insisted that I have two ceremonies—one for the Davidsons, the other for the Chances; she was not going to appear as the fallen woman. When I refused, she decided not to come. She relented a week before the wedding. I hardly spoke to her over the next three years. My rage was heavy to carry.

I wondered about forgiveness. Perhaps it would help. All I needed to do was to say the words, "I forgive you." I didn't even have to mean it.

Once on Pine Street, I began with forgiving myself. There was always plenty to forgive that day or even that hour. By Spruce Street, I moved on to Cassie, my ex-husband, and my siblings. Block after block, I muttered under my breath. Sophie pulled and half charged ahead. Her tail curved over her back, her hindquarters tightly drawn; I followed her bottom.

By 49th Street, I was squarely at my mother and stepfather. A mile from home, I was hot. My arms ached. Turning the corner,

I spat the words like nails, recalling the hurt, humiliation, and isolation: the quiet yearning to belong to a physical body and a family history, the depression I had suffered for years as a child and young adult, the coldness of my stepfather, without a word of thanks or praise, and the flood of grief for Solvig.

I called them names. My hair was wild. I railed. I ranted. I only imagine that I singlehandedly terrorized the whole neighborhood.

That is all I did. I said, "I forgive you." Every morning, for about a year. The words were like bullets, like hail, and then like rain—endless rain. I began to notice things. I was able to be in the room with my stepfather without the oxygen being sucked out. I sat at the dinner table with my mother without leaving in a panic. And a year later, I spent Christmas with them. I received a gift. "Thank you," I said.

Forgiveness is a softening. The rigid rage of my hurt, the little girl stuck between my mother and a man who scarcely knew how to love, began to give way. The anguish of being unnamed and uncalled softened and started to slide off me. Like the earth after a long winter's freeze, I became moist and quiet. The shift was small, the breeze slight, a faint trace of warmth in the air, long-awaited. I let go of the sack; I left the basement.

Forgiveness did not restore love, nor did it create the kind of love I wished we'd had together—that sweet affection of a life-long bond. But it has brought me to kindness. When I visit my mother, I fix lunch. I listen to her. I sit in the kitchen, in the half sun, and bend my head toward her as we drink tea together.

Coda

WHAT REMAINS
BEHIND

My life has been a rich journey out of darkness. Marked by absence, I was, in the end, found by love.

Love is remarkable and durable. Even love lost, love squandered, or love interrupted, it stands by you, silent and strong, until you discover the source. Love is what I stumble on, in the dark, in the half-light, in the glare of the morning rising, in the sweet clearness of the afternoon, and in the blue-gray mist of the setting sun. Love is the lesson, the universe is the book, says the old Sufi saying. And always in action—never in words. The care you take of yourself, your home and family, your work, your community, your city, state, your world. In everything there is love, from the smallest to the largest, in ever-widening circles. From the immediate to the future, love extends out into space.

As I look back, it is not the darkness I fell out of but the love that remains that is remarkable. The sieve of my life has a magical backwardness to it. The mesh allows all rough clumps of dirt and stones to fall through, while the fine rich loam and startling beautiful small stones, wet and glistening from the river of life, remain caught in the filaments.

We are, in the end, a measure of the love we leave behind. While this is no original thought, the experience is always new.

As I write, all primary players of my childhood have aged with dignity and grace. Each loved life and clung to it, not in fear of death but in joy and reverence. Despite physical disability or mental incapacity of age, spring smells sweet.

My father died in 2010, leaving an evanescent trail in his family and in the international science community. (Oh! I miss this good, difficult, complicated, singular man.) My stepfather, unable to take care of himself, finally moved in with my mother. After almost half a century of living apart, they were together again. She cared for him faithfully until he died, making sure he ate well and took his medication, driving him to his many doctor's appointments. When a disagreement erupted, it gave way quickly to animated talk about politics. They did well together.

My mother, now ninety-eight, is tiny from the disintegration of her spine twenty years ago. Bent over, she turns her bright face sideways as she scoots tea and something to eat using her walker as a tray. She sits in her armchair in the small living room surrounded by her books and papers. Her memory is unreliable, but she is always happy to see me.

I call to chat for a few minutes. "How are you doing, Mom?" I ask.

"I'm flourishing!" she laughs, her voice full. Then she grows quiet. "It is a privilege to be alive."

And Solvig? My dear, sweet first mother. Her love and constancy have always been with me—for years unknown. She stood beside me, her hand placed lightly on my shoulder.

"I am here," she said.

She says, "I am always here."

The last time I returned to Sweden in my memory, the day was bright and light filled my therapist's office. Sitting next to me, she took my hand as I closed my eyes and dreamed of how it *could* have been—*should have been.*

The park is dark green, and fir trees line the path. My favorite coat, brown and white speckled, is buttoned up to my chin. My bonnet brim is broad. When I look up, the sky is a curved edge. Terry pulls me along, the sleeve of her coat is black against the white of her hand.

I don't want to be a good girl, I think. I want to be a bad girl. I want to pull away and rush through the doors, up to the elevator, and go home. But I stay.

Eventually we walk slowly down the hallway. The door opens and Solvig kneels to untie my bonnet. "Won't you please take me back?" I cry. "I'll be good! Can't I come back?" She puts her arms around me and lifts me up. I put my face into the soft nook of her shoulder.

"I love you very much, Tina," she whispers, "But Terry is your real mother. We were wrong not to tell you. You were never a bad girl." She holds me tight. "I miss you so much."

The room lightens. I wiggle out of her arms and take her to see the little girl looking out the window. Little Tina is still there, with her nose touching the cold glass. I peer carefully. She might be made of cardboard.

"Let's go outside and play," I say to her. "We can run and play with the boys. Just run around shrieking. We can spin; we can turn around. This is Ulf, and Sven-Johan and Lilla-bror, my little brother.

LET YOUR HEART BE BROKEN

"I miss you all so much. Goodbye Solvig! Goodbye boys! Goodbye Torsten!"

I love you.

My therapist and I were side by side. She put her arms around me as I returned, back into the light of my life. My wet face broke into a smile.

> So easy they say, this birthing
> All it takes is the breath
> Sucking in, hold out
> Let's not talk of holidays or birthdays
> It is long unresolved
> I still love the scepter of soldiers
> Tear blue in the morning
> There is no other ritual for this
> other, this shadow.

> In my own way,
> I still light a candle for that child,
> and call her by name.[1]

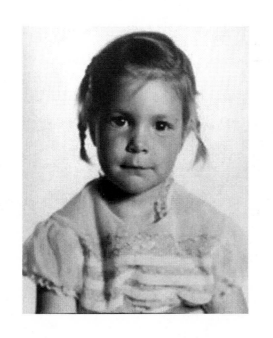

*Sven-Johan, Ulf, Tina, and
Kjell-Olof, Sweden, 1955*

*Sven-Johan, Kjell-Olof, Ulf,
Tina, and Solvig, Sweden, 1954*

Tina, Athens, Ohio, 1958

*Loren, Terry, and Tina,
Key West, 1957*

Tina, Eva, Scott, and Lâle,
Pittsburgh farm, 1965

Tina, Terry, and Eva,
Istanbul, 1961

Loren Davidson, 1966

Britton Chance, circa 1960

ACKNOWLEDGMENTS

The music world is so different from the literary world. As a composer, I sit isolated, dreaming my music into existence. No editor pours over my score to suggest revision or spot errors. No beta listeners are employed to give feedback. Only when the rehearsal process begins do I get an inkling of the nuances and success of the piece before it goes to the audience. I compose and take my chances.

I am grateful for having had so much support in my journey writing my memoir. I am indebted to my publisher, Emily Hitchcock of Boyle & Dalton, for trusting this work, and to my wonderful editor, Heather Shaw, for her expert feedback, enthusiasm, and energy. Finally to Joy Johanneson for her editorial confidence in my writing in its initial phase.

I want to thank my sister, poet, and friend, Eva Davidson, whose gentle suggestions were always supportive of the process. And to my wonderful Cathie Harvey, for her wicked sense of humor and keen eye for typos. To Wood Blum for his steadfast encouragement to finish my manuscript, and Larry Malone for his enthusiasm and advice about publishing.

Thank you, Thais, Tricia, and all my wonderful friends both in Lancaster and Philadelphia for your love and support. To Linda Grace for caring for my body, Augie Hermann and Diane Hunt for generously journeying with me as I dug deep into the emotional content of my past. You lifted me up when I staggered.

And finally, I am grateful for my daughter, Cassandra, for her love and patience, and to my stepchildren, Nora, Noble, and Gabriel.

ENDNOTES

CHAPTER 2

[1] Lionel Nowak (1913-1990), composer & pianist, Bennington College

[2] Louise Glück, "Descending Figure" in *Descending Figure*, (New York: ECCO Press, 1981).

[3] Eva Davidson, *Shadow Grief.*

CHAPTER 4

[1] Erika Jong, *Ms. Magazine*, 1988.

[2] Richmond Lattimore, *Aeschulus 1* (Chicago: University of Chicago Press, 1953), p. 21.

CHAPTER 6

[1] Janice Mirikitani, "Sing with My Body," *Mother to Daughter, Daughter to Mother,* Tillie Olsen (New York: The Feminist Press, 1984) p. 1.

[2] Judith Wright, "Woman to Child," *Mother to Daughter, Daughter to Mother,* p. 3.

[3] Charles Olson, *Maximus to Gloucester: Letter 2.*

[4] T.S. Eliot, *The Love Song of J. Alfred Prufrock.*

[5] Annie Dillard, *A Writing Life* (New York: Harper Perennial, 1998).

CHAPTER 7

1 Oxford American Writer's Thesaurus, p. 928.

CHAPTER 8

1 Joseph Campbell, *The Power of Myth* (New York: Anchor Books, 1988).

2 Elisabeth Kübler-Ross, *Death, the Final Stage of Growth* (New York: Simon & Schuster, 1975), p. 160.

3 Dorothy Dinnerstein, *The Mermaid and the Minotaur* (New York: Other Press, 1976).

4 Grene, D., & Lattimore, R. (2013). In *Aeschylus II: The Oresteia* (3rd ed., p. 60). University of Chicago Press.

CHAPTER 10

1 Stephen Levine, *Meetings at the Edge* (New York: Anchor Books, 1989), p. 57.

2 Stephen Levine, *Healing Into Life and Death* (New York: Anchor Books, 1989), p. 225.

3 Helen Clare, "The Selkie Boy," *Bel and the Giant* (New York: Penguin Books, 1972), p. 30.

4 Joseph Campbell, in conversation with Bill Moyer.

5 Salman Rushdie, *Haroun and the Sea of Stories* (New York: Viking Children's Books, 1990).

6 Helen Clare, "The Selkie Boy," p. 31.

7 James Fenton, "Keeping up with Salman Rushdie," *New York Times Review of Books*, March 28, 1991.

8 Tina Davidson, "Cassandra Sings (Distinctive Voices of Women Composers)," *Ms. Magazine*, 1992.

9 Walt Whitman, *Leaves of Grass*.

[10] Eva Davidson, *Bleached Thread, Sister Thread.*

CHAPTER 12
[1] Linda Schierse Leonard, *The Wounded Woman* (Boston, MA: Shambhala, 1983).
[2] Judith Wright, "Woman to Child," *Mother to Daughter, Daughter to Mother,* Tillie Olsen (New York, The Feminist Press, 1984), p. 3.
[3] Jane Cooper, poet.
[4] Black Elk, an Oglala Sioux medicine man.
[5] Proverbs 29:18.

CHAPTER 14
[1] Thomas Moore, *Care of the Soul* (New York: Harper Perennial, 1994), p. 96.
[2] Sufi saying.
[3] Alix Kates Shulman, *Burning Questions* (New York: Fontana/Collins, 1980).
[4] Coe, R. (1992, July 6). Taking chances. Tricycle. Retrieved from https://tricycle.org/magazine/taking-chances/.
[5] Sri Aurobindo.
[6] John G. Neihardt, *Black Elk Speaks* (Lincoln, NE: University of Nebraska Press, 1979), p 168.

CHAPTER 16
[1] Jeanette Winterson, *Written on the Body* (Visalia, CA: Vintage, 1992).
[2] Anne Carson, *Eros, the Bittersweet* (Princeton, NJ: Princeton University Press, 1986), p. xi.

3   Anne Carson, ibid, p. 111.

4   Anne Carson, ibid, p. 152.

5   Jeanette Winterson, *Written on the Body* (New York: Vintage, 1992).

6   Barbara Kingsolver, *Animal Dreams* (New York: Perennial, 1991).

7   Rainer Maria Rilke, "Sonnets to Orpheus," *The Selected Poetry of Rainer Maria Rilke*, Stephen Mitchell (New York: Vintage, 1989).

CHAPTER 18

1   Sufi saying.

CHAPTER 20

1   Gretel Ehrlich, *Islands, the Universe, Home* (New York: Penguin Books, 1992).

2   Joy Harjo, "Eagle Poem," *In Mad Love and War* (Hanover, NH: Wesleyan University Press, 1990), p. 6.

CHAPTER 21

1   Matthew 22:14.

2   M. Scott Peck, *The Road Less Traveled* (New York: Simon & Schuster, 1978), p. 300.

CHAPTER 22

1   Alice Walker, *The World Has Changed: Conversations with Alice Walker* (New York: The New Press, 2010).

2   Coleman Barks, *The Essential Rumi* (New York: HarperCollins, 1995), p. ii.

3   Joy Harjo, "Eagle Poem," p. 6.

CHAPTER 24

1   Coleman Barks, *The Essential Rumi.*
2   Eva Davidson, "Core of the Earth," from *Billy & Zelda.*
3   Ezra Pound, *Rabindranath Tagore.*

CHAPTER 25

1   Matthew 18:21-22.
2   Clarissa Pinkola Estés, *Women Who Run with the Wolves,* (New York: Ballantine Books, 1996), p. 311.

CODA

1   Eva Davidson, "Shadow Grief."

MUSIC BY TINA DAVIDSON

Page 44   CASSANDRA SINGS (1989) 16' String quartet

Commissioned by the Kronos Quartet, the piece *"builds to a climax of tremendous richness, throwing out a soundscape that would seem to be much greater than merely four instruments can produce. An extended coda achieves a resolution of sublime dimensions."* (Fanfare)

RECORDING; Cassatt; The Cassatt String Quartet, New World Records, 1994

Page 73   BLUE DAWN [THE PROMISED FRUIT] (1989) 10'

Flute, English horn, bassoon, and piano

RECORDING; Tina Davidson: I Hear the Mermaids Singing, New World Records

Page 92   I HEAR THE MERMAIDS SINGING (1990) 10'

Viola, cello, and piano

"Her music is primal. Ostinati knock calmly at the door, and thirds resound like emergency vehicle horns sans the usual impatience and anger. What remains are delightful sounds – sounds that make us human and resound in the universe. If these words sound lofty, it is the result of listening to this otherworldly music." (IWCM Journal)

RECORDING; Tina Davidson: I Hear the Mermaids Singing, New World Records

String quartet

"*The energy and vitality of* Bleached Thread, Sister Thread *creates a sense of journey so palpable and persuasive that the music and poetry flow together in one unified experience.*" (American Music)

RECORDING; Tina Davidson: I Hear the Mermaids Singing, New World Records

Page 161   BILLY AND ZELDA (1998) 90'

9 cast: 5 principal singers (2 sopranos, mezzo-so-
prano, tenor, baritone), chorus, 3 male singers
(TBB), actress/singer, string quartet, improviser
(string instrument), and percussion

Opera in two acts. Lyrics by Eva Davidson and
script by Lâle Davidson.

Page 161   THEY COME DANCING (1994) 15'

Full orchestra

"The freshest piece here was They Come Dancing, *a 15
minute toccata written by Tina Davidson. Ms Davidson
has a vivid ear for harmony and orchestral colors. Over
sustained pedal tones and quietly pulsating bass patterns,
diffuse harmonies – like out-of-focus Copland chords –
sound forth and dance."* (The New York Times)

Page 166   FIRE ON THE MOUNTAIN (1993) 11'

Marimba, vibraphone, and piano

The work *"is rhythmically driving, with fascinatingly simple yet lovely harmonic changes."* (Philadelphia Inquirer)

RECORDING; Tina Davidson: I Hear the Mermaids
Singing, New World Records

TINA DAVIDSON

Page 218   BLESSINGS (SACRED SPACE) (1992) 15'

Solo alto and soprano saxophone and orchestra

"The piece incorporated a primordial, dissonant mutter developed in percussion and bass. Against that, the saxophone plays long low tones, and the player is asked to improvise. It grows towards a clear, bright unison before the piece seems to open into a broadly lyrical, but rhythmically urgent affirmation." (Philadelphia Inquirer)

Page 247   OVER SALT RIVER (1995) 15'

Solo soprano and full orchestra

"The work begins as a lament, but gradually brightens and rises up the scale. This song became a soaring affirmation of the wonder and beauty of life in the face of death." (City Paper of Philadelphia)

Page 253   IT IS MY HEART SINGING (1996) 16'

String quartet and piano or string sextet

"...opens with a wailing, lyrical violin melody – the work is a continuous, meditative swath of sound." (Philadelphia Inquirer)

RECORDING; Cassatt; The Cassatt String Quartet, Albany Records, 2006

311

Page 285   THE DELIGHT OF ANGELS (1999) 18'

String quartet

"a state replete with sweet tunes layered among the strings, fragments that circle in and out of consciousness, sustaining slender, shimmering textures." (Philadelphia Inquirer)

RECORDING; Cassatt; The Cassatt String Quartet, Albany Records, 2006

Listen to music from
LET YOUR HEART BE BROKEN
on Spotify here!

ABOUT THE AUTHOR

TINA DAVIDSON, a highly regarded American composer, creates music that stands out for its emotional depth and lyrical dignity. Lauded for her authentic voice, the *New York Times* praised her "vivid ear for harmony and colors." *Philadelphia Inquirer* writes that she composes "real music, with structure, mood, novelty and harmonic sophistication – with haunting melodies that grow out of complex, repetitive rhythms."

Over her forty-five-year career, she has been commissioned and performed by well-known ensembles such as National Symphony Orchestra, The Philadelphia Orchestra, American Composers Orchestra, OperaDelaware, VocalEssence, Kronos Quartet, Cassatt Quartet, and Grammy award winner, Hilary Hahn.

Long-term residencies play a major role in Davidson's career. She was composer-in-residence as part of the innovative Meet The Composer "New Residencies" and with the Fleisher Art Memorial in Philadelphia. Championing composing in public schools, she created the city-wide Young Composers program to teach children how to write music through instrument building, improvisation, and graphic notation.

Tina Davidson was born in Stockholm, Sweden, and grew up in Oneonta, NY, and Pittsburgh, PA. She currently resides in Lancaster, PA. Learn more about Tina here: tinadavidson.com.

Made in the USA
Columbia, SC
12 May 2023